£4.25

CRIME AND PUNISHMENT

A Study Across Time

Publications by Dr Roger Whiting on crime and punishment:

Prison Reform in Gloucestershire, 1776–1820 (Phillimore)*
A House of Correction, (Alan Sutton)*
Behind Bars – a slide set with detailed notes (Focal Point Audio-Visual, Portsmouth)
Prison Reform – a workbook (Tressell Publications, Brighton)
Prison Reform – an archive simulation game (publication pending)*

Other books by Dr Roger Whiting published by Stanley Thornes:

Religions of Man
Politics and Government – a first source book
To the New World – The Founding of Pennsylvania

*These may be obtained direct from Dr Whiting as the two books are now out of print, and the game is awaiting publication.

CRIME AND PUNISHMENT
A Study Across Time

Roger Whiting, M.A., D. Litt., F.R.Hist.S.
Formerly Head of History,
King's School, Gloucester.

STANLEY THORNES (PUBLISHERS) LTD

First published in 1986 by:
Stanley Thornes (Publishers) Ltd
Old Station Drive
Leckhampton
CHELTENHAM GL53 0DN
England

British Library Cataloguing in Publication Data

Whiting, J.R.S.
    Crime and punishment: a study across time.
    1. Crime and criminals — Great Britain — History 2.   Punishment —
    Great Britain — History
    I. Title
    364'.941   HV6943

    ISBN 0-85950-615-0

Printed and bound in Great Britain at The Bath Press, Avon.

Contents

Acknowledgements

The author and publishers are grateful to the following for permission to reproduce previously published material:

Architectural Press, for artwork from *Prison Architecture* issued by the UN Social Research Institute, published in 1975 (p. 194)

Cambridge University Press, for artwork from *Fabrication of Virtue* by R Evans, published in 1982 (p. 101)

Doubleday Publishers Ltd, for an extract from *Elizabethan Journals Vol 1* by G B Harrison, published in 1965 (pp. 50–1)

E P Publishing Ltd, for an extract from *Prison and Prisoners* by C Lytton, published in 1976 (pp. 199–200)

George Philip & Son, for an extract from *A Social and Economic History* by E H Spalding, published in 1921 (p. 57)

HMSO map reproduced with the permission of the Controller of HMSO (p. 127)

Macmillan, for artwork from *Smuggling* by J Paxton and J Wroughton, published in 1971 (pp. 75, 76 and 163)

Penguin Books, for an extract from *Making of a Nation* by A J Patrick, published in 1967 (p. 79)

We also wish to thank the following who provided photographs and gave permission for reproduction:

Barnabys Picture Library (p. 193)
Batsford (p. 112)
BBC Hulton Picture Library (pp. 21, 27, 46, 73, 86, 91, 92, 108, 114, 118, 132, 133, 168 and 174)
Bodleian Library (pp. 42, 47, 51, 54, 59, 62 and 82)
British Rail, York (p. 111)
Cambridge University Library (pp. 129 and 131)
Central Office of Information (pp. 158 and 160)
J M Dent & Sons Ltd (p. 70)
The Folger Shakespeare Library (pp. 33 and 44)
The Fotomas Index Library (pp. 36, 48, 56, 81, 107 and 137)
Gloucester Cathedral (p. 98)
Gloucester Public Library (p. 102)
Gloucestershire Record Office (pp. 88, 100 and 104)
Gloucestershire Constabulary (p. 154 left)
The Guildhall Library, London (pp. 62, 105)
The Illustrated London News (p. 128)
Library Committee of the Religious Society of Friends (p. 62 left)
The Mail on Sunday (p. 161)
Manchester City Council Local History Library (p. 167 bottom)

The Mansell Collection (pp. 24, 35, 116, 122, bottom, and 203)
Marylebone Public Library (p. 120)
Mary Evans Picture Library (pp. 30, 45, 66 bottom, 64, 78 and 83)
The Museum of London (pp. 66 top, 200 and 202)
National Library of Australia (p. 94)
National Portrait Library (pp. 121 and 142)
Newport Museum and Art Gallery (p. 128)
New Scotland Yard (p. 122, top)
Nottinghamshire County Council Local Studies Library (p. 115)
The Observer (pp. 148, 170–1)
The Photo Source (pp. 154 right, 167 top, and 169)
Punch (p. 106)
D A Rumberlow and Curtis Brown Ltd (pp. 26, 68, 72, 96, 135 and 140)
Service photographique de La Réunion des musées nationaux (p. 7)
Syndication International (p. 187)
Masters and Fellows of Trinity College, Cambridge (p. 28)

Every attempt has been made to contact copyright holders, but we apologise if any have been overlooked.

Note for Teachers

This book is a survey of crime and punishment, and law and order from Anglo-Saxon times up to 1986. It is designed for three purposes: (1) the Welsh GCSE History Module 1; (2) Mode 3 use; (3) any research or long structured essay needed for exam work.

Crime is inevitably with us, and all citizens need to have an appreciation of its causes, methods of containment, trial and punishment. Too often we are influenced by sweeping media statements about living in a lawless and violent age, without realising that things might have been worse in the past. The object of this book is to supply the reader with plenty of factual material, and to use it to pose stimulating questions and to draw attention to trends and developments. A premium is put on empathy throughout.

The layout is basically chronological, and there is a theme guide on p.207 to make it easy to follow a particular subject over the centuries. A limited number of 'Spotlight' sections provide detail of cases that illustrate aspects of the main text. Questions have been arranged to fall at the foot of the page to which they refer.

New museums connected with the police and prisons are opening, and visits to them will no doubt prove rewarding. Mention might be made here of the Beaumaris Prison Museum in Wales, with its treadwheel; Northleach House of Correction in Gloucestershire (part of the Countryside Museum), with its reconstruction trials; and Lincoln Prison chapel, with its cubicles (apply to the Record Office).

The teacher's book which goes with this students' book provides essential back-up material and further questions. Parts of it may be reproduced without permission.

CHAPTER 1

Crime and Early Codes of Law

1. WHAT IS CRIME? WHY ARE LAWS NECESSARY?

Almost certainly you have rules in your own home – about watching television, perhaps, or using the bathroom, or the time for getting in at night. Similarly, there are rules at school, in youth clubs, and so on. For almost everything people do, there have to be *some* rules. They are made for the good of all; without them, there would be chaos. But who makes the rules, and why should members of the household (or school, or club) keep them? These are among the questions we shall be considering in this book.

Though good rules benefit everyone, there are always people who will still try to break them – usually for their own selfish advantage. So there also need to be 'sanctions', or punishments, for people like this.

First, it is essential to agree on what rules there should be. Secondly, there must be someone to see they are applied. Thirdly, there must be a system for judging rule-breakers and giving punishments. Put another way, we have:

a *legislature* or rule-making body (which might be a parent, headteacher, king or parliament);

an *executive* or *administration* (older brothers and sisters, teachers, civil servants, or police) to make sure that rules are obeyed;

and a *judiciary*, or judging system (parents, headteachers, judges, juries or magistrates).

Q1 *Name three rules you have to keep at home. Are the rules in your home the same as in your friends' homes?*

Q2 *Find three rules you have at school which you do not have at home.*

Q3 *How are rule-breakers punished (a) at home; (b) at school?*

Depending on whether we are dealing with a home, a school or a country, the same people may be found in more than one role; but this we will consider later.

So what is crime? *The Concise Oxford Dictionary* says (a) crime is an evil act, a sin; (b) it is an act punishable by law. (Law is a body of rules recognised by the community as binding on everyone. These rules may come from ancient custom; or they may be newer rules 'enacted' by a legislature – in Britain, by Parliament.) Notice that a crime can be one of two things. If it is an evil act or sin, it must be something which is against religious teaching, or at least against human nature. Murder would be one such crime; religions denounce it, and it is generally regarded as an inhuman thing to do. All countries have made laws against such evil actions, so they become 'enacted' crimes too.

But not all crimes are so obvious. Henry VIII ordered his subjects to recognise each of his wives in turn as the lawful queen of the day. Failure to do so meant execution. In this case it was the king's opinion which decided what was a crime; the objectors might have had a different opinion! Things are always changing, as you can see if you think what life was like 2,000 years ago, or 1,000 years, or even 100 years ago. There would be no point in making it a crime to travel faster then 30 mph in a town 4,000 years ago, or even in 1900; but now it is vital for the safety of all.

You will probably have some views on these questions already. But keep them in mind too as you read this book, and see if your views change.

Crimes can be very personal (domestic murders, for example); or affect only a small group (e.g. football hooliganism); or involve a very large group (e.g. suffragettes wanting the vote for women). What crimes of

---

Q1 List any crimes, apart from murder, which you feel are evil acts or sins.

Q2 List any crimes, past or present, which you feel are not actually evil. (For example, is parking on double yellow lines a sin? If not, is it nevertheless useful to have a law against it?)

Q3 Today you hear people saying we live in a wicked age; 'crime is on the increase', and so on. (a) List some crimes which are said to be on the increase today; and say whether you think they involve evil or not. (b) How far is the 'increase in crime' an increase in the wickedness of people today? How far is it an increase in their resistance to laws they just do not like?

Q4 List some things which have always been regarded as crimes; then think of some we have recently made crimes. Is it true that the 'ageless' ones are 'evil acts', while the recent ones are not? Or is this making things too simple?

different kinds often have in common is *violence*. There is domestic violence; local violence when a group tries to impose its authority over another group; and reactionary violence when a group seeks to get back what it has lost (the Peasants' Revolt of 1381 is an example). There is also forward-looking violence, when a group wants something it has never had (for example, the suffragettes). Violence could be seen as a response to social problems such as overcrowding, lack of basic needs, lack of rights, and so on. But many also argue that violence is part of human nature – that it comes from an instinct to survive which is built into mankind. If so, they argue, war is a safety-valve; and when there is no war, the violence will inevitably come out in other ways, such as hooliganism and perhaps even dangerous driving. Of course not all crimes involve violence. Many of those which do not are concerned with *property* (theft is an obvious example).

Thoughts on Crime and Punishment

If you do not prevent a crime when you can, you encourage it. (*Seneca, Roman writer*)

Poverty is the mother of crime. (*Marcus Aurelius, Roman Emperor*)

Steal money, you're a thief; steal a country, you're a king. (*Traditional Japanese proverb*)

You can get much farther with a kind word and a gun then you can with a kind word alone. (*Al Capone, twentieth-century American gangster*)

Prison reform will not work until we start sending a better class of person there. (*Laurence Peter, twentieth-century Canadian writer*)

These thoughts come from different countries, and from several different periods of history. Explain each of them in your own words. Do you agree or disagree with them?

It is possible to think of a number of possible *causes of crime*. Some of them might be:

Poverty. If the cost of living is impossibly high for them, the very poor may turn to crime. Examples might be abandoned and orphaned children in the nineteenth century, or unemployed soldiers after the Napoleonic Wars. (Is this still a cause of crime in Britain today, or has the welfare state made such crime unnecessary?)

Greed. Is this at least one of the causes of shoplifting? Of burglary and theft? Of smuggling? Of fraud?

Hatred, passion, fear. How important are these as causes of murder? Of arson? Of race relations offences?

'Criminal types'. In the nineteenth century, some experts claimed to be able to tell if a person was criminal from the shape of his or her head! This is no longer accepted. But some people do go back to prison again and again. Are they born with a tendency to commit crimes; or is it a matter of the way society treats them?

Crimes can be 'local' to a particular community or country, too. Your town may forbid cars in the main shopping area, while your aunt's town encourages them by putting a multi-storey car park in the middle of the area. In England adults can drink alcohol; but in Iran alcohol is totally banned, as it is in most other Islamic countries.

So whether you commit some crimes can depend on: (a) what period of history you live in; (b) where you live. This means that every community or country must have some procedure for regularly updating the laws it has made. In early days, laws might be made by brute force – the strongest man (tribal chief, king) would simply say what the law was, and if anyone disobeyed, he would deal with them. Perhaps that is the 'law' of your playground today! Alternatively, a priest or prophet, probably supported by the chief, would announce his god's set of laws for the community. Thus Moses and Mohammed presented laws from God (see p.8).

Early laws would be designed to keep the community secure from attack, and stop anti-social behaviour over food and possessions. Selfishness had to be checked, or there would be chaos. Equally, of course, it was necessary to prevent people taking vengeance for imagined crimes, without a proper trial.

In practice, a lot of the law is simply the customs of a society. In England and Wales such law is called *common law*, as it has not been decreed by a king or passed by a parliament. During the Norman period, judges sifted through the customs of the Anglo-Saxons and Normans, and chose the best of these customs to form the common law of England and Wales.

Case law today forms a large part of the common law in England and Wales. In particularly significant trials or *cases*, judges have added a further explanation of the meaning of a particular legal point. (For example, the McNaghten Rules on insane offenders arose from the trial of Mr McNaghten. Case law is built up by the fact that judges follow the doctrine of judicial *precedent*. This means they look back to the interpretations of the law in judgements on similar cases in the past.

Q1   *Try to find three things which are allowed in parts of England and Wales and not in others; and three things which are crimes in some countries, but not in others. Which of these are 'evil acts'? Would the inhabitants of the area agree with your view on this?*

Thus, when a judge hearing a case after the McNaghten one is faced with someone who claims insanity, he uses the McNaghten Rules to decide if the man is really insane or not.

Statute law (*statutum*, Latin for 'I take a stand upon') is produced when Parliament either makes new laws or amends old ones, by passing an Act of Parliament. Sometimes it clarifies points developed by case law. Statute law is the highest form of lawmaking in Britain, as it can overrule or change common law and its case-law developments.

(For example, the McNaghten Rules have now been improved upon by Act of Parliament.)

This book is about criminals, and how the state deals with them under the Criminal Law, for the good of the community. However, today there is also the Civil Law, which enables people, companies or institutions who feel themselves wronged to solve their problems by turning to the civil courts for judgements. The table below explains the essential differences between the Criminal and Civil Laws.

	Criminal Law	Civil Law
AIMS	(a) To protect the community (b) To punish the offenders	(a) To protect individuals and companies, etc., from wrongs done to them (b) To provide a way of settling a dispute between individuals, between companies, or between individuals and companies
PROCEEDINGS	'The Queen versus . . .' Prosecution is in the name of the State; victims may appear as witnesses. The State has a duty to bring criminal cases to trial.	The wronged person or company (*not* the State) brings the case to court. There is no duty to do so; it is up to the *plaintiff* (the individual or organisation claiming to have been wronged) to decide if it will be worthwhile
EXAMPLES OF USE	Murder, assault, theft, arson	Broken or disputed contracts, debts, disputed wills, torts (slander, libel, breach of promise)

Q1 *Can you think of any 'case law' applied when school rules are broken?*

Before we start looking in detail at crime and punishment over the centuries, it is useful to summarise some of the key points we have been considering; it would be a good idea to come back to them from time to time, to see how they apply to particular periods, and whether any of the views we have about them may be changing.

1. One definition of crime is 'an evil or sinful act'.

2. Societies, however, may make some things criminal, even though they are not thought evil or sinful.

3. Some things have always been considered criminal; others are only crimes in some periods, or in some places.

4. Crimes can involve harm to individuals (e.g. murder), groups (e.g. racial discrimination), or property (e.g. theft).

5. Laws can be backed by the authority of:
    (a) religion; (b) long-established custom; (c) a king (or dictator); (d) a parliament, regarded as representing all the people.

6. Laws on crime are made to:
    (a) control crime, and punish criminals; (b) control vengeance (or 'retribution'); (c) ensure all are treated fairly and equally (of course, only *good* laws do this – bad laws may not!); (d) protect people and property; (e) reform the criminal.

7. Possible causes of crime are:
    (a) *poverty* (those who genuinely cannot make ends meet may see crime as their only way out); (b) *greed*; (c) *hatred, passion and fear*; (d) *'human nature'* generally (are we all violent, are some people 'criminal types'?); (e) *'criminalisation'* – making things criminal which were not previously crimes (and should they perhaps not be?).

8. If one believes people are born with criminal tendencies, then cures may be very difficult, and one must simply punish them and protect other people from them. If they become criminal because of their environment, it may be possible to reform them. (Watch out for these two viewpoints down the centuries, and how they affect the way criminals are treated – see especially the material on prisons in the chapters on the eighteenth, nineteenth and twentieth centuries.)

2. EARLY CODES OF LAW

In this book we shall be looking mainly at how the laws of England and Wales (and especially the *criminal* laws) have developed over the centuries. First, though, it is interesting to look at a few earlier 'codes' of law. A 'code' is a systematic collection of laws.

HAMMURABI, King of Babylon in the Middle East, 1728–1686 BC*

*Some readers will know 'BC' as 'BCE' and 'AD' as 'CE'. 'BCE' and 'CE' stand for 'Before the Common Era' and 'Common Era' respectively.

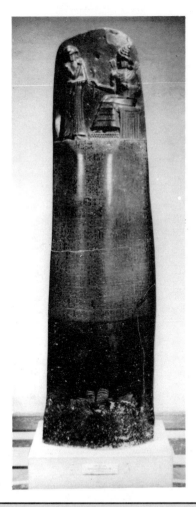

Hammurabi had his laws written on steles (carved stones), and set up in temples. The one placed in the Temple of Shamah at Sippar is now in the Louvre Museum, Paris. It is 2.4 m high and made of polished basalt. On top, the king stands before the throne of the Sun god Shamah (or perhaps the Justice god Marduk). The inscription says the Code was written 'to promote the welfare of the people . . . to cause justice to prevail in the land, to destroy the wicked and the evil. That the strong might not oppress the weak'.

Its 282 clauses, written on 3,600 lines, cover a wide range of subjects. Women are protected and given equal status with men; even slaves are protected. But the Law or Principle of Retaliation for crimes is clear. Possible punishments include death, mutilation and corporal punishment. 'A life for a life' is laid down, though a distinction is made between murder and manslaughter (accidental killing).

The Code of Hammurabi, on a stele

Q1 *Answer the following questions: (a) Who is to benefit from these laws? (b) Who is to be dealt with? (c) Are the aims sensible ones?*

MOSES, Leader of the Hebrews, *c.* 1300 BC

Moses came down from Mount Sinai, and showed the Hebrews two stone tablets on which he had carved 'God's Ten Commandments'. However, these form only a small part of what is known as the Mosaic Law, which is found in the Jewish *Torah* (The Law); they also form the first five books of the Christian Old Testament in the Bible. The Mosaic Law has 613 laws attributed to Moses. It contains the customs and rules of his day. When Ezra read them out from the scroll at the Feast of Tabernacles, it took him from early morning to noon (Neh. 8: 1–9). Notice that Moses attributed the laws to God, making people feel they must obey them.

I
Thou shalt have no other gods before me.

II
Thou shalt not make unto thee any graven image, or any likeness of any thing that is in heaven above, or that is in the earth beneath, or that is in the water beneath the earth: thou shalt not bow down thyself to them, nor serve them: for I the Lord thy God am a jealous God, visiting the iniquity of the fathers upon the children into the third and fourth generation of them that hate me; and shewing mercy unto thousands of those that love me, and keep my commandments.

III
Thou shalt not take the name of the Lord thy God in vain; for the lord will not hold him guiltless that taketh his name in vain.

IV
Remember the Sabbath day, to keep it holy. Six days shalt thou labour, and do all thy work: but the seventh day is the sabbath of the Lord thy God: in it thou shalt not do any work, thou, nor thy son, nor thy daughter, thy manservant, nor thy maidservant, nor thy cattle, nor thy stranger that is within thy gates:

for in six days the Lord made heaven and earth, the sea, and all that in them is, and rested the seventh day: wherefore the Lord blessed the sabbath day, and hallowed it.

V
Honour thy father and thy mother: that thy days may be long upon the land which the Lord thy God giveth thee.

VI
Thou shalt not kill.

VII
Thou shalt not commit adultery.

VIII
Thou shalt not steal.

IX
Thou shalt not bear false witness against thy neighbour.

X
Thou shalt not covet thy neighbour's house, thou shalt not covet thy neighbour's wife, nor his manservant, nor his maidservant, nor his ox, nor his ass, nor anything that is thy neighbour's.

The Ten Commandments of Moses

In any early society, *blood revenge* was a deeply rooted custom (see p.10 for its practice in England and Wales). Relatives had a right to personal vengeance, that is to revenge an injury done to one of their family ('a tooth for a tooth' etc. – see Deut. 19: 21). The Hebrews believed this was part of God's law (Gen. 9: 6).

Q1 *Find out what part of a present-day judge's, barrister's and many Christian clergy's robes commemorates Moses' stone tablets. What is the significance of drawing attention to the tablets in this way?*

Q2 *The Ten Commandments are basic laws, but they have omitted something vital which every criminal law must contain. What?*

THE ROMAN LAW

The Romans were the first to arrange their laws by subject, and to export their laws by taking them with them as they conquered Europe. Their Twelve Tables (451 BC) of laws were originally intended for Roman citizens only, but were then extended to *peregrini* (free non-citizens). They were an extremely well-developed system of law in many ways; they are still studied today, and the Roman code forms the basis of law in a number of countries, including Scotland and France.

The Twelve Tables applied the principle of retaliation ('an eye for an eye' etc.), unless an offender could pay 136 kg of copper for a pardon. Flogging and slavery were among the punishments, and nine crimes had the death penalty:

1. Treason – the offender was veiled, scourged (beaten) and crucified (hung on a cross)

2. Night-time meetings of any kind

3. Murder – if the murderer killed a relative, he was put in a sack with a viper, dog or monkey and thrown in a river

4. Arson – offenders were whipped and burnt

5. Perjury (lying on oath) – those found guilty were thrown from a rock

6. Corrupting a judge

7. Libel – the guilty were beaten with clubs

8. Attacking crops by night – the guilty were punished by hanging

9. Magic

Later laws reserved banishment and beheading for important people, leaving hanging, burning, burying in mines and fighting wild beasts in the amphitheatre for lesser folk.

A Roman was assumed innocent until proved guilty by a court of law. This is a basic principle of English law today, though not of French law. In France, the accused is assumed innocent, but called upon by a court of law to prove his innocence. The 'burden of proof', that is, the task of proving, is upon a French defendant rather than a French court.

CHAPTER 2

The Early Middle Ages in England and Wales

1. PERSONAL VENGEANCE

In the early Middle Ages, personal vengeance, known as *blood-feud* in England and *galanas* in Wales, was a person's basic right. However, there were obvious dangers in this, and gradually the law and the courts began to insist on restricting its use. Anglo-Saxon *dooms* (judgements) tried to reduce the amount of personal vengeance by introducing the idea of Christian forgiveness. At first, though, this only had a limited effect, because a victim's family felt they had a personal duty to revenge the suffering of their relative.

As time went on, more and more restrictions on blood-feuds were made in England. For example, a man could only kill in defence of his lord or one of his relatives; a thief could only be killed if he was escaping with stolen property, or resisting arrest; an adulterer could only be killed by the father or husband of the victim.

In the tenth century, King Edmund's second code of laws also offered *wergild* ('man money') as an alternative to the blood-feud. This meant paying a fine to the relative of a dead person. (If the sum was paid to an injured person, it was called *bot gild*.) The sum depended on the victim's position in society; thus, if you killed a lord, you had to pay more than if you killed an ordinary person.

Q1 *Do other religions, besides Christianity, try to stop personal vengeance?*

Q2 *Write a scene from a play, or draw a strip cartoon, in which a royal official tries to convince a victim's family that they should use wergild as an alternative to blood-feuding.*

Q3 *Organise yourselves into family groups, plan a blood-feud revenge and then discuss whether to accept wergild after all.*

---

2. CRIME PREVENTION – TITHING AND BORH

Before the Anglo-Saxon system of keeping the peace, crime prevention depended mainly on self-help. If you were a victim of theft, you were expected to trace the thief and recover your goods with or without force; if you were murdered, your relatives were expected to track down your killer. In other words, those who had suffered were expected to bring the wrongdoer before the court.

Gradually, the community became involved too, as the start of the *tithing* system in tenth-century England shows. *Hundreds* (a hundred was a group of villages) were made responsible for keeping the peace. Within each hundred, people were organised into associations of ten men called *tithings*, under a *tithingman* (or *chief-pledge* or *borsholder*). Anyone over twelve, unless he was very important, had to belong to a tithing. If any member of a tithing committed an offence, the others had to bring him to court; otherwise they would have to pay compensation to the victim. Any offender who refused to submit to justice was declared an outlaw, and could be killed on sight. When a theft occurred, the victim told the *hundredman*, who was in charge of the tithings, and he called out the tithingmen of the area to pursue the thief.

To support this system of community co-operation, an accused person had to find a *borh*, or *surety*, to guarantee his appearance in court. If the accused failed to appear, the borh had to pay over a sum of money he had pledged as a guarantee. To some extent, the borh system was similar to the bail system of today.

The Anglo-Saxon approach of involving all citizens as part-time keepers of the peace was to last until the nineteenth century, when professional policemen took over the task.

3. TRIALS

Shire and hundred courts were often held out of doors at the *moot* (meeting) place; the monthly meeting of the people involved was therefore called a *folkmoot*. A panel selected from the community leaders heard the cases, under the leadership of the *reeve* or *bailiff* (there were no professional judges then). Later on, the holders of certain property had to act as judges. The victim stated his grievance and swore an oath to his

---

Q1 *Briefly explain (a) tithingman; (b) borh; (c) hundred.*

Q2 *Why was a tithing system practical then, but not today? What advantage did it have over family self-help?*

Q3 *Would it be practical and helpful to make all the people who lived in the same street today form a tithing?*

good faith. The defendant could deny the charge on oath and promise to accept the judgement (*doom*) of the court. The court then decided which of the two had to prove his or her case and by what method. There were three forms of proof:

1. Trial by battle between the two concerned. This was falling into disuse, but was revived by the Normans as we shall see.

2. Compurgation of witnesses; later called *law-wager* in England and in Wales, *rhaith*. The person concerned had to find the number of witnesses (*oath-helpers*) laid down by the court who were prepared to swear that he was telling the truth. This 'proof' did not involve dealing with the facts. The oath of one *thegn* (*thane* or *lord*) was worth those of seven *villeins* (serfs). The size of the oath was related to the amount of wergild which the accused was liable to pay; hence the phrase 'an oath of a pound in value'.

3. Ordeal; an appeal to God to show whether the truth was being told or not.

Let us look now at compurgation and trial by ordeal in further detail, leaving trial by battle to later, on pp.22–4.

Trial by ordeal could involve one of several different ordeals. But before any such trial the person facing the ordeal had to fast for three days and hear mass (communion service), during which he or she was called upon to confess his or her guilt before receiving the sacrament. The priest said to the person:

> 'I charge you by the Father and the Son and by the Holy Ghost, and by
> our Christianity which you have received, and by the holy cross on which
> God suffered, and by the Holy Gospel and the relics which are in this
> church, that you should not dare to partake of this sacrament nor to go to
> the altar if you did this of which you are accused, or know who did it.'

All the ordeals, except the water one, took place inside the church as they were an appeal to God's judgement.

The ordeal by boiling water or oil involved putting one's hand into it to retrieve an object. The arm was then bandaged up and sealed. If it was healed in three days, the person was telling the truth. This was called a 'single' ordeal, but if the offence was serious, a 'triple' ordeal was required. This meant putting the forearm in and not just the hand.

The ordeal by fire reminded people of Shadrach, Meshach and Abednego in the Bible when they were unharmed in the fiery furnace. For a 'simple'

Q1   *Answer the following questions: (a) Why would the bandaging be sealed?*
(b) What was the sacrament which the accused would have received in the
church?

case, the person had to carry a piece of red-hot iron weighing $\frac{1}{2}$ kilogram for three metres, and for a 'triple' case, a larger piece was used. 'Triple' included such crimes as treason, coining, murder and arson. Alternatively, the person would be blindfolded and have to walk over six, nine or twelve red-hot ploughshares.

Only the priest and the accused entered the church, and the priest measured the distance by his steps. Two men were then to enter the church to check that the water was boiling, followed by witnesses who would all be sprinkled with holy water:

> 'And the accused shall drink holy water, and holy water shall be sprinkled on the hand with which he shall carry the ordeal . . . Three steps shall he take to cover the nine feet (three metres), and then cast down the iron and hasten to the altar.'
>
> *(Textus Roffensis)*

For clergymen accused of crimes, there was another ordeal. The accused had to eat the blessed sacrament, for this would surely have choked a sinner. He had to pray that he be choked if he lied.

Finally, there was the ordeal by cold water. This was the most widely used ordeal as water is a pure, god-like element. The person was lowered into the water (see p.22 for directions on this) on the end of a rope in which a knot was made between 'a long hair's breadth' and a metre from the person's waist. If he sank, pulling the knot below the surface, the godly water had received him and he was innocent. If he and the knot floated, the water had rejected him and he was guilty. The ordeal was held near a church to stress the appeal to God and the clergy were paid for administering it. Pope Alexander II frowned on this ordeal in 1070, and the Church finally banned it in 1215. However, this ban was not enforced in England until 1218.

Fines, floggings, the pillory, mutilation, branding, outlawry or death were punishments which could follow failure at the ordeal. Mutilation could include cutting off a hand, foot, nose, ear or upper lip, or putting out eyes. A fine for injuring a person was called a *bot*. Imprisonment was not normally used as a punishment.

SUMMARY

Anglo-Saxon times saw changes from blood-feud to trial by ordeal, and from self-help policing to tithingmen. While the ordeal system involved

Q1 *Choose one of the ordeals and give a vivid description of what it would have been like to have undergone that ordeal.*

Q2 *Why do you think Pope Alexander I disapproved of the cold water ordeal?*

Q3 *Draw a picture of one of the ordeals.*

an appeal to God, tithing involved an appeal to the community. Unwritten laws were added to by the recording of dooms as kings came to exert their authority and pass legal judgements. A beginning to a better method of controlling crime had been made.

4.   LAWS OF HYWEL DDA

Anglo-Saxon law did not extend to Wales. There, during the period when Anglo-Saxon law was established in England, justice was administered under the special code of laws called after Hywel Dda.

Hywel ap Cadell is better known as Hywel Dda ('the Good'). He rather extravagantly claimed that he ruled all of Wales from 942 until his death in AD 950. He is famous as the great lawgiver of medieval Wales. Whether, in fact, it was he or those who came after him, who were responsible for the Code, is difficult to say. The earliest existing copy of his Code of Laws is dated about AD 1200. The copy tells how he called the leading clergy and six men from each sub-division in the country to a 40-day conference about Welsh law. Various changes and improvements were made and issued in book form. Copies in Welsh and Latin exist today.

The Code is very detailed and thoroughly tackles family relations and property, slaves' duties and rights, court procedures, etc. The mystically significant number three and multiples of three like nine figure prominently. For example, there are *three* major categories of crime: (a) homicide; (b) arson; (c) theft. For each crime, there are *nine* possible ways an 'accessory' (helper) can aid the criminal.

Homicide

Accessory's actions	Accessory's penalties	Oath-helpers needed to deny charge
1. Telling murderer where victim is		
2. Encouraging him to do murder	180 silver shillings	100 men
3. Joining in plot		
4. Pointing victim out		
5. Going with murderer on job	360 silver shillings	200 men
6. Going to township concerned		
7. Helping to commit murder		
8. Obstructing victim until murderer arrives	540 silver shillings	300 men
9. Watching murder and not preventing it		

Note that the amounts paid as penalties are multiples of three (*three* × 60; *three* × 120; *three* × 180).

Similar lists are given for arson and theft. As with murder, the accessory may make himself useful to the criminal by one of three methods: (a) his actions; (b) giving advice ('tongue-reddening', as the Code puts it); (c) helping to spot the victim ('eye-reddening').

The murderer had to pay the *sarhad* (penalty) and the *galanas* (value of a person's life; similar to wergild) to the nearest relative. The money was divided into three portions and was paid by (a) the murderer and his family, and (b) and (c) by his other relatives. The first third was paid to the victim's family and the other two-thirds to the victim's other relatives. Clergy, monks, lepers, and mentally retarded relatives of the murderer or the victim were exempt from paying or receiving any galanas. A person who ambushed someone was to pay double *dirwy* (serious crime fine) to the king and double the galanas to relatives.

CHAPTER 3

Normans and Plantagenets

1. THE KING'S PEACE

When William conquered England in 1066 and proclaimed the King's Peace, he meant that he as king was responsible for law and order. It followed that his courts had a duty to deal with serious crime. However, laws had existed in England for over a century before the Normans' arrival, and people did not take kindly to basic changes in their customary legal ways. Realising this, the Normans did not abolish the Anglo-Saxon criminal law system, but established their own system for Normans. Thus, two systems ran side by side for many years, as the supporters of each tried to explain its merits to the supporters of the other.

Under Norman law, 'the King's Peace' could mean different things. This was difficult to understand if you were used to Anglo-Saxon law. For example, if the Normans used the word *frith* for 'peace', it meant a general peacefulness expected in a well-run land. But if they used *mund* for 'peace', then it meant much more. Everyone was entitled to mund around his property and peaceful behaviour from his family and servants. He was entitled to bring anyone who violated his mund for trial. Likewise, the king had a mund linked to his household or court. As he moved around the country, that mund moved with him. By the time of Henry I (1100–35), it covered the whole county the king happened to be visiting. Moreover, particular places, such as highways, great rivers, churches and abbeys, and also such special seasons as Christmas and Easter, were covered permanently by the king's mund or peace. To break the king's mund was more serious than to break that of a householder.

Mund therefore meant both a duty to see peace was kept in an area under your control, and a right to compensation if it was not. The king's mund

Q1 *Can you say: (a) In what ways the head of your home today exercises his or her 'mund'? (b) What form a school's 'mund' has today? What happens if you break it?*

Q2 *Write a dialogue between an Anglo-Saxon and a Norman in which the Anglo-Saxon explains his legal system to the Norman.*

suggests that offences are crimes against the State and not simply against the victim involved. This led to the growth of the idea of crown prosecutions heard by royal judges.

2. THE NORMAN CONQUEST AND THE WELSH MARCH

Having conquered England, William I himself decided to appoint three earls – one each from Hereford, Shrewsbury and Chester – to conquer Wales. Approaching the Welsh mountains from three different directions, these earls conquered the Welsh princes one by one and took their land. This meant they held these lands by conquest, and not as grants (gifts) from the king, and so ruled them as if they were kings themselves. Lesser barons did the same for smaller parts they had conquered. The patchwork of 'states' conquered in this way became the Welsh March. For three centuries Wales was divided into two parts: conquered and unconquered. The conquered part, or Norman manorial (manor-based) area, was ruled first by Norman, then by English, earls. The unconquered part, inhabited largely by tribes, was ruled by Welsh princes. By and large, the two parts co-existed peacefully.

The Black Death in the fourteenth century killed so many Welshmen that law and order in both parts of Wales broke down. When the Welsh Prince Owen Glyn Dwr led a rebellion against the English earls, Henry IV drew up drastic penal (punishment) laws against the Welsh rebels. He ruled that:

1. If any border-town merchant was robbed of his goods in Wales, and the goods were not recovered within a week, the townsfolk could seek revenge on any Welshman they could seize.

2. Welshmen could not get Englishmen convicted of a crime except before an English jury.
These laws were to remain effective until the Act of Union (see pp.39–40).

Glyn Dwr's supporters were declared outlaws. Violent and frequent blood-feuds disrupted life in Wales. Sir John Wynn, describing the chaos, wrote, 'So bloody and ireful [angry] were quarrels in those days and the revenge of the sword at such liberty as almost nothing was punished by law whatsoever happened.'

3. FROM KEEPERS OF THE PEACE TO JUSTICES OF THE PEACE

The origin of *justices of the peace* (JPs) goes back to 1195 when Richard I issued commissions to certain knights to become *keepers of the peace* (*custodes pacis*, in Latin), in the more unruly areas of the land. In 1314 they were given the power to arrest people. In 1327 Edward III ordered that every county, unruly or not, should have 'good and lawful men' to keep the peace. From 1330 *juries of presentment* (see p.20) could report suspects to the keepers of the peace, who could send the accused for trial. In 1344 these keepers of the peace were allowed to sit beside lawyers to 'hear and determine felonies (serious crimes) and trespasses . . . and to inflict punishment reasonably'.

In 1361 the Justices of the Peace Act changed the keepers of the peace into justices of the peace:

> 'In every County in England shall be assigned for the keeping of the
> Peace . . . three or four of the most worthy in the County . . . to restrain
> Offenders and Rioters and to arrest, take and chastise [punish] them . . .'

These JPs had power to bind people over to keep the peace under penalty of a fine and arrest if they broke the peace. In other words, the JPs could threaten unruly people with a fine or arrest before they committed the offence. Indeed, if a person committed the offence while 'under threat', he or she was liable to a fine or arrest before trial. This was a step forward in crime prevention which is still used today.

The increase in the number of JPs and the broadening of their powers, often against the wishes of the Crown, may well have contributed to the growth of freedom in England. The use of local men to administer justice made it unnecessary for the government to put paid officials in all towns, which might have led to the growth of a centralised dictatorship (overpowering rule by one person alone). In their opposition to JPs, the Crown often argued that the JPs were little more than local amateurs when it came to the law. The confusion over who was suitably qualified for the post was settled in 1439. Because men of property were often the best educated and had a special interest in preserving law and order, it was laid down that all JPs should own land producing a substantial income, unless they served in towns.

An act of 1461 made it plain that JPs were now more important than sheriffs. They were to preside at the twice-yearly shire court meetings at which lists were received from the juries of presentment. What would those lists contain?

In the early fifteenth century there were only a handful of JPs in each county, but by the late fifteenth century there were about twenty per county. They came together four times a year for their *quarter sessions*. As juries, local officials, lawyers and prisoners were involved too, it was often necessary to meet in a large place like a castle, or at least a big inn. A session would last about three days. At Huntingdon, on one occasion, armed rioters with ladders tried to break into the room and set fire to it! Crimes of violence, disorderly behaviour at fairs and markets, deceit, etc., were frequently heard by these sessions.

In Richard II's reign, the JPs received attendance pay for each day up to twelve days a year. Except for noble JPs, they had to live in the county where they held their sessions.

4. CATCHING THE CRIMINAL

There was little policing apart from sheriffs in counties, bailiffs in hundreds and reeves in towns. Sergeants of the peace, controlled by royal administrators, covered areas where there was no tithing or *frankpledge* in force, as, for example, on the Welsh border. Frankpledge was the Norman improvement on tithing because the tithing area involved was smaller than it had been in Anglo-Saxon England. Frankpledge also merged tithing with the borh. Males between the ages of 15 and 60 were formed into groups of ten to twelve under their tithingman or *chief pledge* (Norman for borsholder). 'Hue and Cry' was shouted out to the tithing to get them to chase a criminal.

5. EDWARD I'S STATUTE OF WINCHESTER, 1285 – THE SHERIFF'S POSSE COMITATUS

This was the last major law to organise policing until the Metropolitan Police Act in 1829. It updated the list of weapons and armour men in a tithing group had to have ready to serve in the sheriff's *posse comitatus* (an enrolled troop). The list dealt with every item from the poor man's bow and arrows and knife to the knight's armour, sword and horse. The smallest unit of the posse was the *vintenary* of twenty foot soldiers. Two high constables were appointed to each hundred to make a six-month check on its readiness. As the law revived the Anglo-Saxon requirement to join in the pursuit of a criminal, it made every citizen a plain-clothes policeman. The 1285 Statute was an improvement on earlier attempts by Edward I. First, it threatened the hundred with a collective fine if it failed to capture the criminal, even if he fled beyond the tithing area. Previously, the chase had been given up at the town's boundaries. Secondly, it made the tithing group responsible for cutting back brushwood to 200 feet (61 metres) from the royal highways to lessen the opportunity for a criminal to ambush a traveller. Both provisions of the new law stressed the old idea that everyone was involved in maintaining the peace.

Q1 *Why was 'binding a person over' a step forward from the method of making a tithing group responsible for the good behaviour of its members?*

Q2 *Why do you think this property-holding qualification was chosen? What alternatives might have been practical in those days? What qualifications does a JP need today? Does this lead to a wider variety of people becoming JPs today?*

Q3 *What kind of people ought to have been JPs in the Middle Ages, and what kind of people should be JPs today? Think carefully about the structure of your local community when answering.*

6.   JUSTICES IN EYRE

Henry II divided England up into six (later four) circuits with *justices in eyre* (*eyre* is French for 'to wander', hence circuit). Sent out from court to all parts of the country, the justices carried out the king's *assizes* (regulations). Their duties included the setting up of:

A General Eyre – to visit a region to check on crime and policing.
A Commission of Oyer and Terminer (hear and give judgement) – to deal with serious crimes such as treason or felonies.
A Commission of Trailbaston (bâtons were weapons used by riotous gangs) – to deal with violent crimes.
A Commission of Gaol Delivery – twice-a-year circuit to try those in gaols.

When these justices sent by the Crown came to the shire courts, their presence made them into royal court sessions called assizes.

A justice in eyre

7.   JURY OF PRESENTMENT

A criminal could be presented before a court in one of several ways. The victim or relatives could bring a personal accusation or 'appeal' against the suspect and offer to prove it 'by his body' (trial by battle, see pp.22–4). Alternatively, the local community in the form of a jury of presentment (report) could charge the person. A jury of presentment became known later as a *grand jury*.

It should be noted that a jury of presentment, like its successor, a grand jury, only produces a suspicion of guilt. It is not to be confused with the modern (petty) jury which brings in a verdict. What is important is that members of the community can present charges against a fellow member. While awaiting trial, the accused was kept in gaol, which every county had been ordered by the Assize of Clarendon to provide.

8. PRISONS

early prisons

A medieval court of law.

Who is sitting in the chair? How is the accused secured? What is the man at the table doing?

Prisons had existed since Anglo-Saxon times, and by the late Middle Ages had become an important method of keeping order. This was not because they were used much as a punishment given by a court, for that would have cost money, but because they were used to hold suspects awaiting trial.

There was no shortage of people wanting to be gaolers. They knew they could make money out of their prisoners. The whole prison system worked on the selling of services. A good room, heating, light, food, drink and bedding could all be obtained if the prisoner could afford the fees. The fees varied according to the prisoner's importance and ability to pay. In 1356, London City Council issued an order that the chief gaoler at the prison in Newgate refrain from taking unfairly large sums from prisoners in return for services.

9. CHARGING 'BY APPEAL' AND 'BY APPROVER'

Charging by Appeal. This meant a person brought a charge and offered trial by battle with the person he accused.

Charging by Approver. Approvers were people who turned king's evidence by 'splitting' upon other members of their gang. They were hardened criminals who feared conviction or wished their sentences reduced. The king would pay for an approver's keep while he was still in prison.

10. BENEFIT OF CLERGY

The Church claimed that clergy accused of crimes should stand trial in Church courts and not in lay courts. This led to doubts as to who could claim this 'benefit of clergy'. Men hastily tried to plead 'benefit of clergy' when they realised a jury would convict them. Anyone who had a tonsure (monk's haircut) was taken to be a cleric. So a man awaiting trial might have a quick haircut in the gaol to deceive the authorities. By 1350, 'benefit of clergy' extended to holders of Church posts, e.g. doorkeepers, and, by the end of the fourteenth century, to anyone who could read. The reading test was abandoned in the fifteenth century because wider education meant more and more people could read. Sometimes, a prisoner tried to fool the court by learning a Bible passage by heart. One, by the name of John Trotter, was caught out when a suspicious judge handed him the Bible and he failed to notice it was upside down!

11. TRIALS – OATH AND ORDEAL

Proof of guilt still depended upon compurgation by oaths and ordeal (see pp.12, 22–6). The Assize of Clarendon said that the water ordeal was to be used for murder, robbery and other felonies. But the accused would not get this privilege if he had confessed or been caught in possession of stolen goods. In Wiltshire, in 1167, payments were made for 'preparing the pools for the ordeal of thieves'. Holes for the water ordeal were dug near the church. A medieval description of the trial by water read:

> 'Let the hands of the accused be bound together under the bent knees
> after the manner of a man who is playing the game *champ-estroit*. Then he
> shall be bound around the loins with a rope strong enough to hold him;
> and in the rope will be made a knot at the distance of a length of his hair,
> and so he shall be let down gently into the water so as not to make him
> splash. If he sinks down to the knot he shall be drawn up and saved;
> otherwise let him be adjudged a guilty man by the spectators.'

In 1201, in a Cornish burglary case, the judge said, 'Let the males purge themselves by water under the assize, and Matilda by ordeal of iron.' Because of this, women were usually subjected to the ordeal by hot iron and not the ordeal by water.

12. CHOOSING A CHAMPION

Trial by battle was a particularly Norman way of proving innocence or guilt, although it had been used to some extent earlier on in Anglo-Saxon England. It was based on the belief that God decided the outcome of all fights and wars. Consider what people think about such a belief today. Originally, only women, infants and men who were either maimed or over 70 years were excused from the ordeal by battle. Instead they were allowed to choose a champion. Such a champion was probably a relative. Later on, free-lance champions were permitted for trials involving property claims. (Could the term 'freelance' have originated with these champions?)

On the whole, trial by battle was not very common, and usually selected by those accused of treason who feared no jury would acquit them.

In the thirteenth century, a lawyer said that the loss of molar teeth did not enable a person to claim exemption from the trial by battle, but the absence of incisors did! (See below for why teeth used for biting were important.) The set ritual started before dawn in the judge's presence. The combatants, who had been fasting, had to take oaths that sorcery would not be used. A favourite trick was to conceal a written spell on one's person. An approver who had given evidence against a fellow gang member had his head shaven. Both men wore white or red leather clothes. Their weapons were ash staves with iron heads shaped like rams' horns and no armour was worn. Their only means of defence were four-cornered leather shields. The accused had to plead 'not guilty' and throw down a glove, declaring that he would defend it with his body. The accuser picked it up and replied that he would make good the charge 'body for body'. If they broke their weapons, they had to fight on with hands, fists, nails, teeth, feet and legs until one called out 'craven' which was a confession of guilt. The loser was executed.

SPOTLIGHT   SPOTLIGHT

JAMYS FYSCHER 'FISHER AND TAILOR OF CRAFT' VERSUS THOMAS WHYTEHORN 1456

Thomas, a convicted horse thief, had been in gaol for three years on $1\frac{1}{2}$d a day as an approver. He continually named accomplices but none of the eighteen, except Jamys, dared to fight him. The judge 'Master Myhelle Skylling' warned Jamys that he might hang if he beat Thomas who had been useful to the king as an approver. He also told him that if he died he would not be buried in consecrated ground. He ordered them to be dressed in white leather and have metre-long ash staves with iron horns. The fight was to be as 'that most pityfullest judge of all this land in sitting upon life and death' on the 'most sorry and wretched green that might be found about the town' after both had fasted, 'having neither meat nor drink . . . it is too shameful to rehearse all the conditions of this foul conflict; and if they need any drink they must take their own piss'.

The crowd was for 'that true man, Jamys Fyscher' and tried to get the judge to string Whytehorne up before the fight began! This was rejected and the approver came 'armed out of the East side' and the defendant 'out of the Southwest side in his apparel', to kneel and pray to God and the world for forgiveness. The crowd all prayed for the defendant. This exasperated Whytehorne, who called out mockingly to know why Jamys was making such a long show of his false belief . . . Jamys jumped up and swore that his quarrel was as sincere as his belief, lunged at Thomas, unfortunately breaking his weapon in so doing. Thomas fought on, gaining the advantage, until officials succeeded in disarming him. A brief pause for breath followed. Then unarmed combat began. 'Then they bit with their teeth, that the leather of clothing and flesh was all rent in many places of their bodies. And then the false approver cast that meek innocent down to the ground and bit him by the member, that the poor innocent cried out'. By luck Jamys managed to get up onto his knees and grabbed Thomas by the nose with his teeth 'and put his thumb in his eye'. Thomas called for mercy and the judge stopped the fight.

Trial by battle. Describe the weapons and shields used. Have the men any armour?

Both were told to retell their tales, Thomas finally admitting he had wrongly accused Jamys as well as 28 others and begging for mercy. 'And then he was confessed and hanged, of whose soul God have mercy, Amen.' Jamys, who might legally have been executed for plotting the death of someone who had given King's evidence, was 'pardoned his life, limb and goods and went home'. He became a hermit and 'with short time died'.

Q1 *Interview either Jamys or Thomas and get his views on all that happened during the ordeal by combat.*

Q2 *What part did the spectators play in this case? Should 'the community' become involved in a trial? Give your reasons for and against.*

Q3 *Do you think justice was done? Why? If your answer is yes, would you still think so had Thomas won?*

13. THE PETTY JURY

In the twelfth century, it was felt that while the ordeal was too crude and barbaric, compurgation was too open to lies and deceit. If they were to be abandoned, this would leave the problem of how to prove guilt or innocence. Gradually, this was done by the accused being asked to accept the verdict of a jury of twelve of his or her neighbours. There was a charge of one mark for this alternative. This jury was not the jury of presentment (later called the grand jury), but what became known as the *petty jury*, from the French word *petit*.

In the days when the juries were being introduced to try cases, some members of the jury of presentment might be put on the petty jury. On some occasions, all the members were. Later on, people showed their dislike of the 'charging' jury being turned into the 'judging' jury and they were finally kept separate by an act of 1352. In that year Edward III agreed that no one was to serve on a petty jury if challenged by the accused. The first task of these juries, which comprised twelve to thirteen (or sometimes nine to sixteen) men, was to act as detectives to find out all they could about the accused. As they were acting as law officials charged with obtaining evidence, their names were published so everyone knew of the duties.

Threatening or bribing a jury was known as *embracery*. It was all too common. In 1468 Chronicler Stow wrote:

> 'This year divers [many] persons being common jurors were sworne for rewards or favour of the parties, were judged to ride from Newgate to the pillory at Cornehill with mitres [bishops' hats] of paper on their heads and then again to Newgate.'

Until the fourteenth century, a jury's verdict did not have to be unanimous. Juries were reluctant to convict neighbours of a felony as that meant a death sentence. Those who were most likely to be found guilty were those caught in the act or with the stolen goods on them, and notorious characters and strangers.

It was essential to get the accused's consent to the trial jury procedure as it was at first not considered as trustworthy as the God-controlled ordeal procedure. The question was put, 'Culprit, how will you be tried?' The answer, 'By God and my country.' The fact that he said 'and my country' indicated his acceptance of a jury trial.

From 1275 by the 1st Statute of Westminster, notoriously bad people who refused a jury trial were faced with *prison forte et dure* (soon changed to *peine forte et dure*). This meant imprisonment with weights placed on one's chest while lying flat on the ground, 'as much as he could bear and more',

---

Q1 *Are names of modern jury persons published? If not, why not?*

while being given only mouldy bread and stagnant water on alternate days. This would continue until he agreed to plead before a jury or died. A sharp stone was put underneath his body to break his back. Some men would deliberately endure the agony until death. In this way, they avoided the confiscation of their property that went with being found guilty of a felony. This form of legal torture did not end until 1712.

In Henry II's reign courts made more of an effort to obtain evidence to get at the truth than they had under trials by oath or ordeal. Ranulf Glanvill showed this when he wrote:

'The truth of the matter shall be investigated by many and varied inquiries and interrogations, and arrived at by the considering probable facts and possible conjectures both for and against the accused who must in consequence be either completely absolved or made to purge himself by ordeal.'

Peine forte et dure. How is the prisoner held down? Is there anything that suggests this picture was drawn just before the torture was abolished?

14. THE KING'S COURTS PROVIDE BETTER JUSTICE

Petty juries were only available when a justice came round on circuit, and were never used in manorial courts. This meant that the English kings could offer better justice than the Norman ones. On the other hand, early petty juries were chosen not because they were impartial (not biased), but because, as local men trying a local man, they often had a better knowledge of the facts. Although they were not eye-witnesses of the crime, they were encouraged to find out the facts by their own private inquiries. Their verdict had to be unanimous, and they were denied food and drink during their discussions. Too often, corrupt sheriffs chose jurymen to aid one of the parties involved in the case.

Two criminals are publicly whipped through the streets to prison in 1370. Why will the criminals' feet hurt when they reach the prison? Which official is on horseback?

15. PUNISHMENTS

In medieval times, there were two aims behind punishments: (a) *deterrence*, making a person frightened to do a similar crime; (b) *retribution*, making a criminal suffer for the wrong he had done. Notice there was no thought of reforming the criminal. Thus when the Norman period began the aim was to make the punishment fit the crime: hanging for murder; burning for arson; cutting out the tongue for slander or false accusation. But the Normans themselves did not make the punishment fit the crime. William I abolished capital punishment in favour of mutilation (although Henry I later restored the death penalty with its idea of an 'eye for an eye'). In any event, punishment remained harsh. The Assize of Clarendon ruled that if one lost the ordeal, one would lose a foot and be given eight days to leave the country on pain of outlawry. The Assize of Northampton increased this to the loss of the right hand as well as a foot.

In addition to public hangings and floggings of both men and women, other public punishments were inflicted. The pillory had been used in Anglo-Saxon times, and people who used false weights and measures, or committed fraud, perjury, or libel received this punishment. Sometimes their heads were shaved too. The stocks were used less frequently. The Statute of Labourers, 1351, required stocks to be set up in all villages as 'open gaols' where runaway servants and labourers could be held until claimed by their masters.

The stocks. Why was this 'open gaol' punishment a better deterrent than imprisonment?

In 1406 an act said that every town must have a set of stocks for drunkards, profaners (someone who treats something sacred with contempt), gamblers and vagrants (wandering unemployed).

Imprisonment was not seen to be as strong a deterrent as public executions and whippings seen by all, because prisoners were kept in gaol and out of sight. If someone was sentenced to prison, he or she would get one or two years on average, though sentences could vary from weeks to life. In Edward II's reign larceny involved a week in prison for every penny's worth stolen and three days for every halfpenny's worth.

16. OUTLAWRY

Someone who was outlawed was at anyone's mercy if caught in the land. An outlawed woman was called a *weyve*. An outlaw had to swear, 'I shall go forth from this realm of England and shall not return thither again except with the license of the lord king or of his heirs, so help me, God.' The outlaw had to put on a pilgrim's sackcloth and set out barefooted. Carrying a cross, the outlaw headed directly for a named port. Enough money was given for the journey.

In Richard I's reign the price on an outlaw's head was the same reward as offered for killing a wolf, five shillings (25 p). In fact one's chances of avoiding capture were considerable. Later medieval kings were eager to pardon outlaws in return for money or for their doing military service. By the mid-fourteenth century it was the normal practice for justices alone to put a captured outlaw to death. William Speke of Spalding in 1397 did not realise this when he cut off the head of an outlaw and he had to receive a pardon for his deed.

17. SANCTUARY AND CORONERS

Running to a church – *seeking sanctuary* – was one manoeuvre open to criminals. This gave them immunity from arrest for a week and sometimes longer in abbeys holding famous relics. Westminster, Glaston- bury and Beaulieu Abbeys' sanctuaries also covered a mile (about 1.6 km) radius around them with stone crosses marking the protected areas. Pursuers could be fined according to how far they had passed these stones. The aim was to give time for a settlement to be reached between the accused and the accuser. This stressed the Christian idea of mercy. The accused hoped that the accuser would swear not to demand the extreme penalty so that he could look forward to his trial with hope. Certain criminals were denied sanctuary, namely traitors, heretics, sorcerers, clerks, outlaws and those with a criminal record.

On arrival the person had to confess to a priest and surrender his weapons. He was then under the clergy's control and his name, address, job, confession and the victim's name were registered. In some abbeys he would be fed, but in most parish churches this depended on the good will of the priest. Men from the four nearest towns had to keep watch on the sanctuary and they were fined if the person escaped. Three or four days later the coroner would come to hear his confession and his promise to leave the realm. If the person refused to make this promise he would have

> **Q1** *Why do you think outlawing someone was a practical punishment in those days, but not today?*

to surrender himself for trial within 40 days. If the person refused to stand trial, he or she would be automatically convicted and either forcibly removed or starved out.

There were so many complaints about this custom of sanctuary between 1315 and 1316 that Edward II made a law ordering that the:

> 'coroner shall cause . . . the felon be brought to the church door, and there be assigned to him a port, near or far off, and a time appointed to him to go out of the realm, so that in going towards the port he carry a cross in his hand, and that he go not out of the king's highway, neither on the right hand, nor on the left, but that he keep it always until he shall be gone out of the land; and that he shall not return without special grace of our lord the king.'

An escapee seeks sanctuary. How can you tell the man is an escapee? Who are the men receiving him?

By the end of the fifteenth century people were branded with an 'A' for Abjuration of realm on their thumbs which meant they had sworn (abjured) to leave the kingdom. They set out dressed in white sackcloth with a red cross on, barefooted and bareheaded. No one was allowed to molest them. Men from the four nearest towns acted as escorts. Times for their journeys into exile varied. In 1295 the Norwich coroner gave one man three weeks to go 180 miles to Portsmouth and another man four days to go 170 miles to Sandwich. Work out their average speeds! On arrival they had to seek a boat leaving on the next tide. If no ship was available they had to wade into the sea up to their knees each day for up to 40 days and then return to the sanctuary to await the news of a ship's arrival.

The right to sanctuary was not always respected. A sensational case occurred in 1378. Robert Haulay, having escaped from the Tower of London, was slain in Westminster Abbey where he had taken sanctuary from a band led by the Tower's constable. Mass was being celebrated at the time. The killers were excommunicated (expelled from the Church) and fined heavily. The Abbey was closed for some months and had to be reconsecrated (re-blessed). In 1454 the Duke of Exeter was taken out of the Abbey in spite of the abbot's protest. Nevertheless, sanctuary-seeking was widely practised. Between 1464 and 1524 those rushing to Durham Cathedral included 195 murderers, sixteen debtors, nine cattle thieves, seven thieves, four prison escapers, four horse thieves, four housebreakers, and others numbering in total 243. Most sanctuary seekers *did* leave the kingdom.

Henry VII began to put a stop to sanctuary-seeking and Henry VIII ended it by closing the abbeys.

Q1 *Draw the story of Robert Haulay in a series of cartoon pictures.*

Q2 *Make up a short story in which a criminal seeks sanctuary and then has to answer to the coroner.*

Q3 *Write an argument between a monk explaining the Christian idea of mercy behind sanctuary and a sheriff trying to arrest a murderer.*

CHAPTER 4

The Tudors

1. NEW TREASON LAWS

To make sure that nothing like the Wars of the Roses occurred again, the Tudors were determined to make the *rule of law* apply to all. Harsh justice was to be handed out. New courts were created to make sure that justice dealt with powerful persons as well as common men. MPs and lawyers joined forces to make sure Parliament was the supreme law-making body whose laws were to apply to all.

Henry VIII became the first English monarch to make the clergy subject to the king's law. As a result, he and his Tudor successors became supreme rulers over the Church in England as well as the State. A string of new treason laws were passed, widening the meaning of treason. Admittedly the 1352 Treason Act was very out of date. It simply said that treason was bad personal behaviour towards the king as feudal overlord, and that it was not a political offence at all. It listed three categories of treason: (1) attacking the king's life; (2) helping his enemies; (3) waging war against him. It did not say that to imprison or depose a king was treasonable!

Henry VIII's new laws said it was treason to speak or write against the king and his current wife and heirs, or to support the pope. Anyone who claimed that the king held beliefs which were against the normal teachings of the Church or used his power unjustly was committing treason. Even keeping silent when questioned on what were the king's rights and authority was taken as treason. This meant that political opinions as well as political acts could be considered treasonable.

> **Q1** *What do you think is meant by the 'rule of law'? Give any recent examples of people or groups defying it.*
>
> **Q2** *Give three examples each of deeds which (a) any community would take as crimes; (b) would be crimes only if a ruler made them so.*
>
> **Q3** *Is it essential for a ruler to make certain deeds into crimes if he is to rule effectively?*

Freedom of opinion was gone. Religious as well as political beliefs were involved in this clampdown. Countless people lost their lives as a result of these laws.

London Bridge. Notice the gate shown in the picture. Why put traitor's heads on it?

2. COPING WITH RETAINERS

A widespread cause of crime was the use barons made of their private armies of *retainers* (followers) dressed in their *livery* (uniforms).

But how was a powerful man with his retainers to be tamed? In the 1570s Lord Chandos had used armed retainers in Gloucestershire to protect his servants who had been accused (probably rightly) of highway robbery! Using retainers for corrupt purposes was clearly possible too. The answer to how to curb the abuse of retainers was a strong court in London where a powerful man would not be able to make use of his local influence, where there was no jury to corrupt, and where torture, not allowed in the common-law courts, could be used against anyone accused of a crime. For a short period an act of 1487 (later rather misleadingly called the Star Chamber Act) permitted special court meetings by some of the King's Council to take place in a room called the Star Chamber. (The room got its name either because there were stars painted on the ceiling or because it was where 'star' agreements were stored.) In fact the so-called 'Star Chamber Court' was simply the King's Council meeting on Wednesdays and Fridays from 9 a.m. to 11 a.m. in this room to do judicial business. People could be summoned to it to answer certain matters on oath by *writs* (official orders) sealed by the Privy Seal of the king. Thus the accused could be questioned without knowing really what the charge against him was.

The Star Chamber Court also dealt with matters not properly covered by acts of Parliament or the common law; for example, conspiracies, perjury, or interference with the courts' hearings. The Star Chamber Court's punishments were not controlled by acts but as the Court thought fit. They ranged from heavy fines to pillorying, ear-cropping, nose-slitting, branding and whipping. The Star Chamber Court could not give the death penalty. The Court was abolished in 1641 by the Long Parliament which thought it helped rulers to govern as dictators.

Having forbidden the keeping of private armies of retainers or liverymen, Henry VIII was furious to see 500 retainers lining the Earl of Oxford's driveway when he said farewell to the Earl after a visit. Turning to the Earl, he said, 'By my faith, my lord, I thank you for your good cheer, but I cannot endure to have my laws broken in my sight. My attorneys will speak with you.' The Star Chamber made the Earl pay 15,000 marks. It was an enormous fine for the time.

Sometimes new 'crimes' were created by rulers to serve their own ends. Bitter arguments over whether the pope and the Roman Catholic Church should be recognised in England or whether the new Church of England under the sovereign was to be the state Church, led to the passing of many laws in the Tudor period. In those days freedom of worship did not exist; one had to use the form laid down by the ruler or suffer the consequences. In Henry VIII's and Elizabeth I's reigns failure to accept the Church of England was taken as treason and the punishment was execution. Under Edward VI and Mary I failure to toe the line (the Protestant line for Edward, the Catholic for Mary) was heresy and led to

Q1 *Why would some frustrated citizens welcome the Star Chamber Court's work?*

Q2 *Why might other frustrated citizens object to the Star Chamber Court's work?*

Q3 *Do countries in the world today pass laws which remove an individual's freedom to have any religious beliefs he or she likes?*

burning the body so as to free the soul and allow it to ascend to heaven. A treason charge allowed the ruler to confiscate the property of the accused so perhaps Henry and Elizabeth made more profit from the charge of treason than Edward and Mary did from the charge of heresy!

Four heretics are burned to death at Smithfield, London. What kind of people are on security duty for the burning? What do you suppose the man in the round stand is doing?

JOHN MADELEY CASE HEARD BEFORE THE STAR CHAMBER

A typical case involved John Madeley of Quixhill, Staffordshire, prosecuting his neighbour, John Fitzherbert of Derbyshire, in 1496. The latter had claimed some of Madeley's land as his own and had his men harvest it. Madeley got a judgement against Fitzherbert in the local court but instead of handing over the corn he and his men stole six cows and a horse from Madeley. So Madeley got a Bill of Complaint lodged at the Star Chamber which explained the violence done. He asked for a Privy Seal writ against Fitzherbert.

'To the King our Sovereign lord, and to all the noble and discrete
[prudent] lords of his most honourable Council.

'Showeth meekly unto your Highness' noble and sad [grave]
discretions, your humble and true liegeman and orator [petitioner]
John Madeley, of Quykkeshull in your County of Stafford, that where
[whereas] John Fitzherbert of Norbury in your County of Derby,
Esquire, . . . the ninth day of February in the ninth year of your most
noble reign, come to Quykkeshull aforesaid, with eight persons in
his company, to your beseecher unknown, and then and there break
up the doors of your said beseecher, and entered into his house,
and there took out and drove away six cows and a horse, and them
drove to Glaxton, and there . . . impounded them [put them in the
pound] by the space of five days where through the horse died,
without any offence or trespass by your said beseecher to him done,
and the cows he kept. . . . Please your said Highness, of your most
noble and abundant grace, and your noble and sad discretions . . . of
your gracious and blessed disposition . . . by the advice of your
discrete lords, to grant your gracious letters of Privy Seal . . . to the
said John Fitzherbert . . . commanding him upon his allegiance to
appear afore your grace, and the noble lords of your Counsel, to
Answer to the premises . . . and this for the love of God, and in the
way of charity.'

Fitzherbert was ordered to appear by the Lord Chancellor, and the
Keeper of the Privy Seal sealed the writ and sent it off by
messenger. When he appeared before the Star Chamber
Fitzherbert was told to put his answer in writing:

'This is the answer of John Fitzherbert Esquire to the Bill of
Complaint of John Madeley.

'The same John says that the said Bill is insufficient and
uncertain . . . But for declaration of the truth he says that [the house
and land belonged to him], . . . and the same John Fitzherbert . . .
came to Quyksull aforesaid with three of his daily servants, as he
most commonly uses to walk, and then and there found a horse and
six beasts damage feasaunt [doing] in his own Freehold, by force
whereof the said John took the said horse and beasts . . . and them
lawfully impounded . . . by the space of one day and one night, and
that . . . they were deliverd to the said John Madeley . . . safe and
sound.'

All these and the other points in his defence, Fitzherbert declared
himself ready to prove:

'As your gracious lordships shall think reasonable, . . . and he
prayeth to be dismissed with his costs and charges for his wrongful
vexation and trouble.'

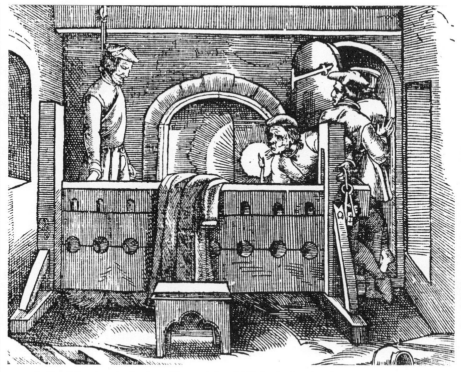

An English prison in the time of Queen Mary I (1553–8), showing the torture of a Protestant bishop by suspension by an iron neckband, allowing his toes to touch the ground.

Then Madeley sent in his reply and Fitzherbert replied to that. The interrogation followed when Fitzherbert had to answer questions on oath. In the meanwhile three abbots who lived near the two men were told to interrogate local witnesses. They found blind 80-year-old Richard Wener who swore that Madeley was the tenant, not the owner of the land and that Fitzherbert's father had bought it. When this and other evidence had been considered the Councillors each gave their opinion and the judgement depended on the majority's views. Unfortunately the judgement has been lost. Who would you have decided for and why?

The Star Chamber, despite its drawbacks, did please many who wanted justice to be the same for all throughout the country. In Elizabeth I's reign it was the most popular court in the land. William Lombarde said in 1591, 'this most noble and praiseworthy court, the beams of whose bright justice . . . do blaze and spread themselves as far as the realm is long and wide'.

3.   HENRY VII'S LETTERS OF DENIZENSHIP AND CHARTERS OF ENFRANCHISEMENT

Following his victory over Richard III at Bosworth, in 1485, Henry VII rewarded many of his Welsh followers with letters of *denizenship*(admittance of foreigners to a resident's rights). This meant they were given the rights and privileges of Englishmen and were no longer subject to Henry IV's penal laws for the Welsh.

In 1505 he began issuing charters of *enfranchisement* (freedom) to some lordships and then to the principality of North Wales in 1507. Thus all Welshmen were equal in law with Englishmen and Englishmen could be tried by Welsh juries.

4.   ROWLAND LEE, PRESIDENT OF THE COUNCIL OF THE MARCHES OF WALES

Lawlessness continued in Wales for several reasons. First, juries failed to convict powerful magnates (local rulers) of their crimes either out of fear or because they were bribed. Second, murder went unpunished except by the Council of Wales. Third, the custom magnates had of befriending criminals who were often relatives on the run for cattle stealing. This custom was called *arthel* or *advowry*. Fourth, magnates forced people at gatherings called *commorthas* to pay fines owed by the magnates for their crimes.

Thomas Cromwell, Henry VIII's right-hand man, decided on strong action to improve the situation in Wales. The Bishop of Lichfield and Coventry, Rowland Lee (died 1543), was made President of the Council in 1534 with power to order executions. Although a clergyman, he had never preached and much preferred to lead his men in chasing cattle-thieves. He was told to stop crime in the Marches, the border area between England and Wales. He had little love for the Welsh. As a brutal, fearless and energetic man, he was ideal for the job in Henry's eyes. He enjoyed punishing criminals and boasted that he had ordered the hanging of 'four of the best blood in the county of Shropshire'. However it is doubtful whether he hanged 5,000 in his six years as President of the Council, as Chronicler Ellis Griffith claimed.

In 1576 William Gerard wrote:

> 'This stout bishop's Dealing . . . within three of years generally so terrified them as the very fear of punishment rather than the Desire or love that the people had to change their Welshry wrought first them the obedience they now be grown into.'

Henry supported him with a string of emergency laws. In 1534, it was decreed:

1. Juries suspected of giving false verdicts were to be severely punished by the Council;

2. No night-time crossing of the River Severn was permitted in order to stop cattle raids from Wales into England;

3. No one was to carry arms, and arthel and commorthas were forbidden;

4. All offenders escaping from a lordship had to be returned;

5. Marcher lords' officials were to be tried by the Council if they wrongfully imprisoned or fined people;

6. Crimes committed in the Marches could be tried in the nearest English county. This meant that English JPs tried Marcher criminals rather than leaving them to the Marcher lords to deal with.

Between 1536 and 1543 a new policy to promote friendship between England and Wales was put into force. There was to be a union between the two countries. Rowland Lee was not consulted. When he heard that there were to be Welsh JPs under the new arrangement, he protested they would be the very men who befriended thieves! But the fear of a foreign invasion of England through Wales, the need to enforce the Reformation, and the desire of the Welsh for union meant he had to be ignored.

Union was brought about in three stages: 1536, 1541 and 1542–3.

1536

Two acts were passed in this year. The first said eight JPs were to be appointed in each Welsh shire. They did not need to have the £20 a year qualification required in England. The shires were divided into hundreds fitting the old *commotal* areas of administration. The second act for 'laws and Justice to be Ministered in WALES in like Form as it is in this Realm' was an act of union blessed by Henry's 'Zeal, Love and Favour' for the Welsh. It was to make Wales part of England. It abolished the rights and privileges of the Marcher lords and ordered that English law be applied. Welsh men could then stand for Parliament, but were only allowed to hold office in Wales if they could speak English. Unfortunately it was a rather hasty, confused act, but it did appoint two commissions (inquiry committees) to fix boundaries and report on whether to keep any of Hywel Dda's laws. It allowed Henry to suspend or revoke it in three years if it did not work properly.

1541

Four justices of assize for four circuits were appointed under this act.

1542–3

This act gave the Council of Wales and the Marches wide powers over Wales, and the English counties of Herefordshire, Gloucestershire, Worcestershire, Shropshire, and Cheshire. It could hear all criminal cases brought to it by people too poor to go to the common-law courts; it tried serious offences and heard appeals from lower courts which it supervised. It was abolished in 1641. A Court of Great Sessions was also established under the act to take place twice a year for six days at a time in every shire. The assize judges who ran these sessions could try all serious crimes. Quarter Sessions were to be held by the new JPs while sheriffs were to hold monthly County Courts and hundred courts every fifteen days for minor matters. The sheriffs' position was downgraded; in future they were to hold office for one year only and were placed firmly under JPs' control. They were put in charge of county gaols for the first time. But their bailiffs were reduced to supervising executions, pillories and whippings. Constables of the peace were appointed in each hundred. They were under the JPs' control. In addition the act also provided that sheriffs were to hold twice-yearly *tourns* (a check-up on frankpledge) and arrest anyone charged by juries of presentment. The new JPs were exempt from the minimum property qualification of £20 a year. A fresh stage in Welsh history had begun. It ended the powers of the Marcher lords to rule and try people. All Welshmen were now on an equal footing with Englishmen. The new system of rearranged courts was cheap and speedy, and it lasted until 1830.

5. TUDOR JUSTICES OF THE PEACE

Meanwhile, in England the Tudors were relying more and more on their country gentlemen assistants, the JPs. In fact local government and local law and order depended upon them. William Lambarde wrote a 600-page book on the job of being a justice of the peace in 1602. The average country gentleman was by that time in possession of a £20 a year freehold and could qualify for the post. A JP's religious views were noted and he had to take the oaths of supremacy and allegiance which meant that he recognised the monarch as head of the country and Church. By the end of Elizabeth I's reign 309 acts of Parliament affected JPs. Henry VIII required them to supervise inns, regulate alehouses, maintain bridges, apply regulations on weights and measures and deal with vagrants. Under Mary I the maintenance of roads was added, and under Elizabeth I the whole direction of poor relief, the regulation of manual workers' wages and the establishment and management of houses of correction which provided compulsory work for the unemployed.

An act of 1530–1 to deal with the alarming increase of robberies and theft ordered that, 'any person, being whole and mighty in body and able to labour, found begging or being vagrant and giving no satisfactory account of how he or she lawfully obtained his or her living' could be arrested by a constable. A JP could have him or her stripped naked, tied to a cart and whipped 'till his or her body should be bloody'. The vagrants then had to swear to return to their birthplace or where they had lived for the last three years and there 'labour as a true man ought to do'. Notice how people who were unemployed but fit to work were made into criminals by being idle or begging.

A vagrant on his way to prison. Is the man who is being whipped being dealt with correctly according to the law? What do you think is the reaction of the onlookers? Would this be a sensible punishment today and, if so, for what crimes?

The 1572 act for the punishment of vagabonds and for the relief of the poor and impotent (helpless) opened with these words:

> 'Where all parts . . of England and Wales be presently with rogues, vagabonds and sturdy beggars exceedingly pestered, by means whereof daily happeneth . . . horrible murders, thefts and other great outrages . . . be it enacted [that any over 14 years old] be brought before one of the justices of the peace . . . and be presently committed to the common gaol . . . there to remain . . . until the next sessions of the peace or general gaol delivery'.

Anyone then found guilty was whipped and burnt through the 'grisle' of the right ear with an inch-thick 'hot iron'.

Q1 *What did the act assume was the cause of begging?*

JPs had to compile a register of the 'poor, aged and impotent' and then tax the community to raise money to care for them. They were to appoint overseers of the poor to specialise in poor relief. The 1576 act for setting the poor to work instructed JPs to buy work materials and provide 'houses of correction' in which vagabonds were to be 'strictly kept as well in diet as in work, and also punished from time to time'.

A gaoler from an engraving from Mynshul's Essays and Characters of a Prison. How has he made sure his keys are safe? Do modern prison officers do the same?

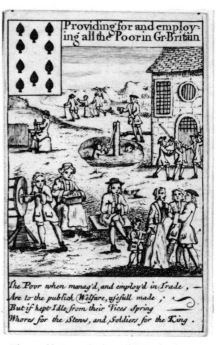

The workhouse solution. This card refers to Lawrence Braddon's idea for starting a company to specialise in the care of the poor, but it shows a house of correction. Note the water pit; those in it had to keep pumping to prevent drowning. If people drowned it proved they were lazy! This was used in Amsterdam's workhouse.

SPOTLIGHT   SPOTLIGHT

TUDOR ROGUES

The London underworld was more highly organised than the local policing system of the day. Some parts such as Damnation Alley and Devil's Gap were 'safe' areas for criminals. The criminal fraternity (brotherhood) saw to the allocation of tasks, operational areas, disposal of stolen goods and the systematic training of recruits. Read what William Fleetwood, Recorder of London, wrote in 1585:

'There was a school house set up to learn young boys to cut purses. There were hung up two devices, the one was a pocket, the other was a purse. The pocket had in it certain counters and was hung about with hawk's bells and over the top did hang a little sacring [communion] bell; and he that could take out a counter without any noise was allowed to be a Public Foister [pickpocket]; and he that could take a piece of silver out of the purse without the noise of any of the bells, he was adjudged a Judicial Nipper [cutpurse].'

Some underworld specialists:

Abraham man – one who pretended to be mad
Angler, curber, hooker – a thief who hooked things from open windows using a folding device which looked like a walking stick
Bawdy basket – female pedlar
Charm – lock-picker
Cog – card or dice cheater
Counterfeit crank – pretended to be epileptic
Cutpurse – cut purses from people's belts
Dummerer – pretended to be dumb
Foin – pickpocket
Padder – highway robber
Ruffler – one who claimed to be an ex-soldier

Some underworld language:

Beak, queer-cuffin – a magistrate
Budge a beak – to flee from the law
Headborough – constable
Gilks – skeleton keys
Black art – picking locks
Clog – steal
Bung – purse, pocket
Nip a bung – cut a purse
Cony – victim
Fullams – weighted dice
Darkmans – night-time
Queer-ken – prison

Pamphlets were frequently issued to warn country visitors to London of these people. When walking in St Paul's Cathedral 'approach not within 5 fathom of that pillar but bend your course directly to the middle line'. Cutpurses used to hide behind pillars.

John Selman, a notorious cutpurse, who was arrested on Christmas Day, 1611, for cutting the purse of a servant of Lord Harrington's in the chapel in Whitehall and in the King's presence. He was executed a year later.

How did JPs cope with all this? In Suffolk they divided the county into areas and appointed 'foreign officers' to patrol fairs, markets, etc., to spot vagrants and then get the local constable to take them to the nearest JP. If they were committed to a house of correction ('bridewell', after the original house of correction, Bridewell), then the constable was paid a small sum per mile to escort them there. On arrival adults got twelve lashes of the whip and youngsters six strokes on their bare backs. If necessary the vagrant was manacled (chained).

Bridewell. This was built as a palace but Edward VI gave it to London in 1553 'to be a workhouse for the poor and idle persons in the City of London'. What does its size suggest about the extent of the unemployment problem?

6.   MAGISTRATES' CRIMINAL WORK

Before 1554 JPs could only arrest people on definite charges. After 1554, they could arrest people on suspicion, interrogate them for three days – much as a detective would today – then, if need be, commit them for trial. At these felony examinations the person who arrested the accused, as well as his accusers, had to appear. If the JP felt the accused had a case to answer, he noted 'the examination of the said prisoner and information of them that bring him, of the fact and the circumstances thereof for certification to the next gaol delivery'. He then bound the accusers to give evidence at the trial and committed the accused to prison. If two JPs were present the prisoner could be granted bail.

Persons committing misdemeanours, such as drunkenness and brawling, could be dealt with 'summarily' (without a full trial) by a single JP, often in the JP's own house.

Two or three JPs met to hold Petty Sessions to deal with minor offences, but four times a year the bench would meet for Quarter Sessions. At such meetings a group (*quorum*, meaning minimum number required) of the most experienced or legally trained JPs had to be present. One of the

Q1   *Why do you think one JP alone was not allowed to grant bail?*

quorum was appointed as *custos rotulorum* (custodian of rota) to take charge of the writs, presentments (reports) and indictments (charges). A clerk to the justices acted as the court's legal adviser and business manager. Quarter Sessions could handle murder, assault, theft, witchcraft, poaching and rioting among other charges. They could not deal with treason, and in practice the more difficult or serious criminal cases were heard by the judges of assize anyway. They commonly awarded floggings and frequently hangings.

The ducking stool was used for scolding or gossiping women until as late as 1819.

> 'If noisy dames should once begin
> To drive the house with horrid din,
> Away, you cry, you'll grace the stool,
> We'll teach you how your tongue to rule'.
> *(Ben West)*

Ducking a scold in the local pond. Make a model of a ducking stool.

JPs received an allowance on the days they sat. They did most of their administrative work dealing with the poor, tavern licensing and arranging road repair during the Quarter Sessions. Among other things they could suppress unlawful games such as football.

'Batchelor's Triumph', from the Roxburghe Ballads. *Who is encouraging the man to play? Why do you think there is a tankard on the table?*

7. CONSTABLES AND WATCHMEN

Constables were appointed by Quarter Sessions. The high constable of a hundred became in effect a servant of the JPs. Appointed for between three and ten years, he faced a heavy fine if he refused to serve. In Wales, under an act of Henry VIII, he had to be a substantial yeoman or a gentleman, and this was usually true in England too. He had to report to the JPs on the state of the roads, on the pubs and on any *recusants* (Roman Catholics) or vagrants. He also received the poor relief money from the churchwardens and passed it on to the JPs. Naturally he relied on the petty constables for his information. These men now operated in villages as well as towns. All male adults were compelled to do this unpaid work for a year from time to time, although they often paid someone else to do it for them. This meant that, in some places, almost permanent 'professionals' were now at work. Their duties were noted by William Lambarde:

> 'First, in foreseeing that nothing be done that tendeth either directly or by means, to the breach of the peace; secondly in the quieting and pacifying those that are occupied in the breach of the peace; and thirdly, in punishing such as have already broken the peace.'

They had to use their own initiative, such as they had, and make regular presentments (reports) to the court. They had no uniforms or weapons. All able-bodied males were obliged to do service at night as town watchmen. They too had no uniforms or weapons.

O per se O.

OR

A new Cryer of Lanthorne and Candle-light.

Being an Addition, or Lengthening, of the *Bell-mans* Second Night-walke.

In which, are

Difcouered thofe Villanies, which the *Bell-man* (becaufe hee went i'th darke) could not fee : now laid open to the world.

Together

With the fhooting through the arme vfed by counterfeit Souldiers:
The making of the great Soare, (commonly called *The great Cleyme* :) The
Mad-mens markes : Their phrafe of Begging : The Articles and
Oathes given to the Fraternitie of Roagues, Vagabonds, and
fturdy Beggers at their Meetings.

And laft of all,

A new Canting-Song.

Printed at London for *Iohn Bufbie*, and are to be fould at his fhop

A woodcut from the title-page of a pamphlet. The bellman patrolled the streets. 'Remember the clocks. Look well to your locks.' He is carrying three things. What uses could he make of each?

8. PUBLIC ORDER

The dictatorial rule of the Tudors, their insistence on their subjects worshipping in the way they themselves did, and poor economic conditions leading to much vagrancy, brought outbreaks of rioting and revolt from time to time. To add to the Tudors' problems, there were attempts to overthrow them by plots and uprisings. How did the Tudors cope with these threats?

They began to use secret agents to spy and to intercept mail. Their agents were also prepared to plant evidence when need be. The success of their secret service can be seen by the way Mary, Queen of Scots, was finally trapped in the Babington Plot of 1585. Tudor spy-chief Walsingham's agents tricked Mary into thinking she had a safe mailing system using the weekly beer-delivery cart; then they used the evidence they had acquired to convict her of treason.

Government agents also had to cope with the problems of hunting down Jesuit priests smuggled into England in Elizabeth I's reign to promote the Catholic faith. The agents were up against the cleverness of Nicholas Owen who devised numerous 'priests' holes' in houses where priests could be hidden.

Other arrangements were needed to cope with mass uprisings such as the Pilgrimage of Grace in 1536, the rebellion of Kett in 1549 and that of Wyatt in 1554, to say nothing of rioting apprentices. The sheriff could call out the *posse comitatus* or militia, but more was needed than that. Nobles were appointed as lord lieutenants in each county. In fact they took over the military powers of the sheriffs. Each had two deputy lieutenants to aid him. They were often the leading JPs of their counties and they had to select the best men available for training, check their equipment and see that they were ready for action.

When a serious riot or uprising occurred the sovereign issued a proclamation imposing martial law (virtually military rule). There was a provost martial in each county who had to see that order was carried out.

Q1 *Answer these questions: (a) If you were Nicholas Owen, where would you try to construct a hiding hole in a house? (b) How big would it have to be? (c) How would you conceal the entrance to it?*

Q2 *If you were a government spy checking up on hidden Jesuits, where would you look in a house and what investigation techniques would you use to find a hiding place?*

Q3 *What role do lord lieutenants and deputy lieutenants have today?*

TEENAGE APPRENTICE RIOT, MARTIAL LAW PROCLAIMED IN LONDON, 1595

The background to what follows was: first, a greedy, unscrupulous Lord Mayor; second, a food shortage; third, a large number of unemployed men pretending to be soldiers.

June 13: Many apprentices, short of food, who were paid only 3d instead of 5d, stole butter in Southwark Market.

June 15: The Constable locked some in the Counter Prison because they had denounced the Lord Mayor.

June 16: Apprentices met some 'soldiers or masterless men' in St Paul's area and 'the soldiers said to the prentices, "You know your strength." Then the prentices asked if the soldiers would assist them'. The soldiers agreed, saying 'they would play an Irish trick with the Lord Mayor, who should not have his head upon his shoulders within an hour'.

June 23: 'About 4 o'clock . . . some prentices . . . being sent to Billingsgate by their masters to buy mackerels and finding none there', heard the Southwark fishwives had bought the stock from the boats. 'Hereupon the prentices, in number 60 or 80, pursued after them, without any weapons, having only baskets under their arms; and coming to the fishwives they took their mackerels . . . giving them [the correct] money . . . Then one of the fishwives began to lay about her and offered to strike some of the prentices with her fish basket; but when the constable, seeing the disorder, commanded these rude and unruly persons' to disperse they did so.

June 27: 'The riotous prentices' who had taken the butter a fortnight earlier were whipped, put in the pillory and then imprisoned.

June 29: On Sunday afternoon 'a number of unruly youths on Tower Hill' attacked the warders of that ward (see pp. 56–9) with stones. Many were then arrested by the sheriffs.

July 4: Royal proclamation forbad unlawful assemblies, and imposed a night-time curfew, and officials were told to enforce law and order.

July 18: Provost-Marshal appointed. 'Elizabeth by the grace of God, &c., To our trusty and well-beloved servant, Sir Thomas Willford, Knight, greeting. Forasmuch as we understand that of late there have been sundry great unlawful assemblies of a number of base people in riotous sort . . . although . . . sundry offenders [have been] committed to several prisons; and have also received corporal punishment by direction . . . of our Council in the Star Chamber . . . Yet, for that the insolence of many of this kind of desperate offenders is such as they care not for any ordinary punishments . . . we find it necessary to have some such . . . persons . . . speedily suppressed by execution to death according to . . . martial law; and therefore we have made choice of you . . . to be our Provost-Marshal, giving you authority . . . to take the same persons; and in the presence of the said justices, according to . . . martial law, to execute them upon the gallows . . . And furthermore we authorise you to [go] with a convenient company into all . . . highways . . . where any vagrant persons do haunt, and, calling to you assistance . . . our justices and constables [living there] . . . to apprehend all such vagrant and suspect persons and them to deliver to the said justices . . . [and] you shall by our law martial cause to be executed upon the gallows . . . some of them that are so found most notorious.'

July 24: 'Five of the unruly youths' involved in the June 29 disturbances were 'drawn from Newgate to Tower Hill, where they were hanged and bowelled as traitors'.

July 25: 'In London, such is the scarcity of victual [food], that an hen's egg is sold for a penny . . . a pound of . . . butter for a penny.'

The persecution of Catholics by Protestants in an English prison in 1587

Q1 *Write a newspaper article about recent teenage rioting in London, 1595. Do not forget to include an interview with a rioter and another with the Provost-Marshal.*

CHAPTER 5

The Stuarts

1. THE DIVINE RIGHT OF KINGS

Religion and politics continued to be hopelessly tangled up in the seventeenth century. Kings claimed God had selected them to rule – a theory called the Divine Right of Kings. This meant they could do no wrong and must be obeyed by all as they represented God on earth. Thus their decisions could overrule those of their courts and they were quite prepared to dismiss judges who did not do as they were instructed.

Judges in eyre not only dealt with court cases, but had to see that the king's political and administrative business was carried out too. They had to report back the local reactions to the king's orders. The Star Chamber Court became a harsh instrument of the king's power. Torture was freely used to aid its work. Political trials called *impeachments* involved the House of Commons prosecuting the accused before the House of Lords who acted as jury and judge combined.

There was a system for releasing people who had been detained without charge, trial or sentence. It was called *habeas corpus*, which translated meant, 'you have the body'. These were the opening words of a writ sent to a gaoler ordering him to produce the body, dead or alive, before the judge who sent the writ. In this way the judge could find out if a person was legally detained or not and release the person if need be. If the gaoler did not obey the writ he could be imprisoned! The force of *habeas corpus* was seriously weakened under the Stuarts when judges heard the Case of the Five Knights in 1627. The Knights had been detained for failing to loan some money to the king. The Knights applied for a writ of *habeas corpus*. The judges, fearing dismissal, ruled that anyone arrested on the king's command could not apply for the writ. They said no cause for an arrest was needed for such 'matters of state'.

Q1 *How could the claim of Divine Right of Kings affect crime and law and order?*

Q2 *Why is the* habeas corpus *writ so important for the liberty of a citizen?*

This case and others led to a breakdown of good relations between the King, Charles I, and Parliament. The King was forced to agree to abolish the Star Chamber Court and its Church equivalent, the Court of High Commission. Despite these concessions things only got worse and Civil War followed between the Cavaliers and the Roundheads. The outcome was a mockery of a trial of the King by so-called 'commissioners' in which he was condemned to death for waging war against his subjects. God's chosen ruler, fountain of law and order, was executed by his people.

Soon the victorious Roundheads were forced to maintain the peace by establishing martial law. The country was divided up into eleven districts with a major-general and 500 troops in charge of each. Juries were 'packed', newspapers suppressed and good behaviour insisted upon. Swearing became a crime. Fines were less for a commoner (i.e. a non-noble) than for a duke. Failure to pay meant anything from three to six hours in the stocks. The justice imposed by the victorious Roundheads became very unpopular. In the Restoration that followed, most people welcomed Charles II back to the throne.

Religious strife, however, did not cease with the Restoration. There were heated arguments over whether Charles's younger brother, the Catholic James Duke of York, should succeed him. The arguments led to a series of genuine and fictitious plots. The fictitious Popish Plot of 1678, the suspected Meal Tub Plot of 1679–80 and the genuine Rye House Plot of 1683 resulted in numerous trials and executions. Different plots were often portrayed on sets of playing cards. Each of the 52 cards showed what happened or was claimed had happened.

James II dismissed judges and magistrates to suit his aims, believing it to be his duty to enable people to be Catholics freely and openly. His carefully selected judges agreed that the king could appoint Catholics as army officers so he could gain political control of the army. But his pro-Catholic actions led to him being chased from the throne in the Glorious Revolution of 1688. In William III's reign which followed, Parliament insisted on passing the Act of Settlement, 1701 (its full title was 'an act for the further limitation of the Crown and the better securing of the rights and liberties of the subject'). It stated that judges should not be

---

Q1 *Under the Roundheads 'unnecessary' taverns were closed, horse racing was stopped and Father Christmas forbidden. How far should a government control the leisure activities of its citizens? Should people engaging in leisure activities that cause no harm to others be regarded as 'criminals'? Is it ever justified for a government to make laws against engaging in leisure activities?*

Q2 *What kind of offences might you commit that would make a judge who feared for his own job treat your case unfairly?*

S^r. E.B.Godfree is perswaded to goe down Somerset house Yard.

S^r.E.B.Godfree Strangled Girald going to stab him.

Ireland and Grove drawn to their execution.

Pickerin Executed.

Playing cards describing the Popish Plot of 1678. Magistrate Godfrey was mysteriously murdered after Titus Oates told him the Plot. Those executed were not in fact the murderers.

removable unless Parliament petitioned the king. This meant that judges could apply the law without fear of a king (or, today, a prime minister) dismissing them out of hand. This was a big step forward in English legal history towards making trials fairer.

2. STUART JPs

James II realised that JPs had a lot of influence in parliamentary elections, and he sent them a list of political questions to answer to find out if he could trust them. Of the 1,311 JPs, 203 turned out to be Catholics. The remainder were Protestants and critical of his aims. Wholesale dismissals followed and half the lord-lieutenants were sacked too. Replacement JPs included one who could not read or write and another once convicted of manslaughter!

Such tampering with justice only encouraged the people to want a revolution against the king. Because Stuart kings often appointed their supporters as JPs there were complaints about 'justices of mean degree' (men of humble origin) replacing 'men of stature' (prosperous, leading figures). These new JPs had to seize every opportunity to collect fees or accept bribes as they were not wealthy enough to live well otherwise. In the countryside they were known as 'basket justices' because they kept huge baskets handy for offerings. Town JPs were nicknamed 'trading justices' as they were mere tradesmen. Oliver Cromwell had tried to improve the standards of judges while he was military dictator, but his work was undone during the Restoration.

In James I's reign, the JPs had been grouped in regions to do preliminary investigations like detectives. Because a JP had to look after the poor and bridges, etc., as well as deal with criminals, his work load became too heavy and he grew careless. To prevent this, when he came to the throne, Charles I issued a Book of Orders to make it clear what the JPs' duties were. This book, together with reports JPs were now required to make, led to Petty Sessions as well as the Quarter Sessions meetings becoming an essential part of the local government system.

Q1 *Why do you think James II appointed unsuitable men as JPs?*

Q2 *What were the advantages and disadvantages of appointing 'men of stature' as JPs? Do not forget to consider what type of people they had to judge.*

Q3 *Find out what type of people are selected as JPs today. Who selects them?*

Sir William Bromley, Warwickshire JP

Sir William kept a notebook to record his 'out-of-session' work done in his parlour, which he called his 'Justice Room'.

'1691. 7 Feb. On the complaint of . . . Norton of Kenelworth, mercer, that his daughter Sarah lives an idle, disorderly life and pilfers his goods. Sir W. Broughton and I committed her to the house of correction.

1691. 8 May. Alexander Barlow of Brincklow, alehousekeeper, swore the peace against Gervase Ledgely of the same, carpenter, for beating him and threatening to burn his house.'

JPs had to make their petty constables bring them lists of:

1. Names of Popish recusants;
2. Names of regular drunkards and innkeepers permitting drunkenness;
3. Names of those who swear profanely and how often;
4. Names of those neglecting watch and ward duties;
5. Names of those not helping to repair roads;
6. Names of bakers selling light bread, etc.

The disruptions of the Civil War led to JPs being largely free from control. For two hundred years they came to run the countryside in the interests of people like themselves – 'the propertied classes' – rather than those of the whole community. This meant the poor were often unprotected. (We shall see how this led to much restlessness in the late eighteenth and early nineteenth centuries.) In Charles II's reign JPs got the additional power to appoint special constables in emergencies. Further difficulties with policing arose when there was no proper supervision of petty constables or the watch and ward.

THE HIGGINSON FAMILY AND THE LOCAL CONSTABLE, JANUARY, 1682

'Mr Higginson sent [to the constable] . . . to come again to his house or his son would kill some of them . . . and coming into the house . . . [the constable] commanded . . . Samuel Higginson to be quiet . . . his father offered to thrust [Samuel] forth of the house and Samuel pushed his father back . . . Mr Higginson said to the [constable] 'you must be rough with him and take him to the stocks'.'

A further report went on:

'William Williamson, one of the constables of Castle Northwich . . . saith that . . . William Vernon of Castle Northwich . . . called him . . .

to come to Mr Higginson's house . . . to keep the king's peace, for Samuel Higginson of Northwich . . . was then in his father's house fighting and quarrelling . . . and would not be ruled. This examinant seeming unwilling to go . . . Vernon further charged him in the king's name to come and assist him set . . . Higginson in the stocks, whereupon this examinate went . . . [and] commanded peace in the king's name, which was observed in his sight, and . . . Williamson went home again.'

Constable Williamson's report:

'Mr Higginson said [to the constable] 'you must be rough with him and take him to the stocks' . . . whereupon this examinate laid hands on . . . Samuel Higginson and desired him to be quiet, and . . . Samuel spurned him on the left shin . . . Peter Worrall . . . a neighbour . . . laid hands on . . . Samuel to aid this examinate . . . to take him out . . . this being done, this examinate released . . . Samuel and did forbear taking him to the stocks at the desire of his father and mother.'

SPOTLIGHT

SPOTLIGHT

'A Watch is to be kept in every Town, Parish, Village, and Tything, every night from Ascencion till Michaelmas, from Sunset to Sunrise, which the Constables, etc., must constantly cause to be set, and that by two or four men, according to the greatness of the place. These Watchmen are to apprehend and examine all strangers that pass by them in the night, and if they find cause of suspicion in them, then they may secure them till the morning, and if the parties refuse to obey the Watchmen, they may levy hue and cry to take them, and upon their Resistance the Watchmen may justify the beating of them, and set them in the stocks or Cage [timber cell] till morning.'

A writer in 1677

Q1   As William Williamson, the constable in the Higginson family Spotlight, make your report to the local JP in modern English. Then, as a JP, list the questions you would put to the Higginson family and say whether you think anyone should be punished and how.

Q2   In France kings appointed their own agents to administer justice rather than rely on local JPs. Which is likely to be the better legal system and for whose sake?

If a riot occurred JPs turned first to special constables then to the sheriff's *posse comitatus* and finally to the militia. In 1662 the militia was put under Crown control. Lord-lieutenants were ordered to aid JPs when local riots got out of control. This meant a total force over the country of 93,000, incuding 6,000 mounted men, was available. In London JPs also had the use of four regiments consisting of 6,000 trained men.

The post of Provost-Marshal, begun by the Court of Aldermen (senior councillors) of the City of London in 1570 to deal with vagrants, was developed in the seventeenth century. There were two marshals, the Upper, and the Under or Second. Each was in charge of six 'young men'. The marshals had to purchase their jobs, as so often happened in those days. By 1712 the purchase price was ten times a year's salary. The marshals received clothing and horse allowances and a sum for each person committed to a London prison. In addition, they were paid a protection fee by every stall operator at the crime-ridden Bartholomew Fair (see p.70). They and their assistants were thus a regular paid force, working alongside the constables and watch. But they had more power because they could arrest people in counties beyond London, and, later on, in the whole of England.

In seventeenth-century England apprentice rioting was connected with holidays. In 24 out of 39 years (1603–42) there were riots on Shrove Tuesday involving thousands in the London area. Catholics, especially Spaniards, were picked upon in such ritual rioting. Brothels and playhouses were always attacked, their windows broken and the occupants and officials assaulted. Demobbed, unpaid forces joined in. Unpaid sailors were a constant threat. Rioters were whipped, fined and imprisoned, and on a few occasions, executed.

Possibly the first example of the use of militia to stop rioting was described by Samuel Pepys on 24–5 March 1668, when London apprentices rioted and pulled down houses. He wrote that:

> Lord Craven, in charge of the troops was 'riding up and down to give
> orders, like a madman . . . And we heard a JP this morning say to the
> King, that he had been endeavouring to suppress this tumult, but could
> not, and that, imprisoning some of them in the new prison at
> Clerkenwell, the rest did come and break open the prison and release
> them'.

This use of the militia was rare in the seventeenth century, but it was to become more common in the eighteenth century. By the early nineteenth century the regular army was involved too in the maintenance of law and

---

Q1   *Bank holidays' 'Mod' style rioting occurs in seaside towns today. Would it help if they were punished in the way that rioters were in seventeenth century? Why or why not?*

order. Something must have gone sadly wrong with the social, economic and political life of the nation in that period for this to happen.

Two cards from a pack on the 1688 Revolution showing mobs attacking Catholic embassy chapels: Palatine chapel in Lime Street on October 29, and the Mass house at St John's on November 12.

3. CRIMINAL HEARINGS

Some improvement in court cases was made in the early Stuart period. Prosecution witnesses usually came into court instead of the clerk reading their *depositions* (sworn statements). The prisoner would not know what they would say in advance, but he could refuse to answer questions and was allowed to cross examine witnesses and call his own too. However, it was possible to hire 'men of straw', men who would witness to anything they were paid for. They would hang around the courts indicating their availability by straw stuck in their shoes. A new practice of turning king's evidence, though somewhat similar to the old approver system (see pp. 21–4) grew up with an offer of a pardon if one gave evidence against a prisoner.

There were no rules of evidence. Prosecution witnesses could mention details of the prisoner's past life, for example, which might prejudice the case against him. Hearsay evidence was allowed. As it was the custom to complete a case in a day, a trial could last late into the evening. Judges summed up very briefly and were occasionally very harsh, as is shown by Judge Jeffreys dealing with the Monmouth rebels.

THE MONMOUTH REBELLION OF 1685

James, Duke of Monmouth, attempted to seize the throne in 1685 from his uncle, James II, the Catholic king who was finally forced to flee the country three years later. Monmouth's rebellion failed at the battle of Sedgemoor and Monmouth himself was beheaded in London. He told the executioner, Jack Ketch, that the axe was not sharp enough when he tipped him six guineas. He was right. The first stroke only wounded his neck. He made no sound, but looked Ketch in the face. The second blow was no better. Monmouth crossed his legs in pain. After the third blow, Ketch threw down the axe and cried, 'God damn me, I can do no more'. The sheriffs ordered him to carry on while the crowd threatened to lynch him. He succeeded at the fifth stroke. Monmouth's head was sewn back on to his body and he was decently buried.

In the West Country Judge Jeffreys was ordered to punish the rebels. The task was a large one. Some 331 men were executed, 849 transported and 33 whipped or fined. It was soon called the 'Bloody Assize'.

The three of clubs shows men hanging in chains at a road junction. Such a punishment was exceptional and could only be ordered by the king as a warning to others. The queen of hearts shows the execution of Alice Lisle, an old widow, at Winchester. She was accused of hiding two rebels in her house, although in fact she did not know they were there. Her house was known as a centre of the nonconformist get-away underground system. The jury retired three times before convicting her. She was sentenced to be burnt, but was beheaded in the end.

After 1688 judges became less biased. Rules of evidence and procedure came to be set which helped prisoners in their defence. Hearsay evidence was discouraged. From 1702 prisoners on felony charges could get their witnesses to speak under oath and from 1708 those on treason charges were given a list of prosecution witnesses and jurors ten days before their trials.

Grand juries of professional men, landowners, etc., still presented the accused before the courts. But petty juries no longer had to have a direct knowledge of the accused, or the crime, before the trial. From 1705 they did not have to come from the accused's home area.

Q1 *How would these changes affect the petty jury's attitude to a prisoner? Would they help or hinder the jury in reaching a decision?*

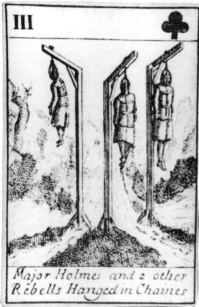

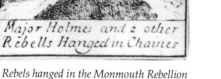

Rebels hanged in the Monmouth Rebellion   The execution of Alice Lisle

Jurors were liable to be punished if they failed to convict when a judge directed them to do so. But in 1671 when Edmund Bushell and his fellow jurymen refused to convict William Penn, the Quaker, of holding an unlawful meeting, in spite of their being locked up for 48 hours without food or drink, fined and then imprisoned, they were soon released on a *habeas corpus* writ.

After 1689 juries were not punished for their verdicts. If they could not reach a verdict, they were discharged and a fresh trial held with a new jury.

'Benefit of clergy' had become a farce. The mere *reading* of part of Psalm 51 verse 1 (nicknamed the 'neck verse') was changed to *reciting* it from memory in 1705. Although many criminals claimed this exemption, more offences were made 'non-clergyable' ones. In 1692 women were allowed to plead 'benefit' for any first charge of felony they faced.

> The neck verse:
> 'O loving and kind God, have mercy.
> Have pity upon my transgressions.'
> *Psalm 51 verse 1*
> The judge asked, *'Legit aut non legit?'* ['Does he read or not?']
> The cleric replied, *'Legit ut clericus'*. ['He reads like a cleric']

Q1   *Explain fully how a* habeas corpus *writ got Bushell and his fellow jurymen released.*

Because the number of felonies carrying the death sentence went up, more and more prisoners faced execution. Transportation to Maryland and Virginia increased after it became an alternative to death in Charles II's reign. The pillory was increasingly used for political offences. In 1632 William Prynne had both his ears cut off and was pilloried, fined and imprisoned for life for writing an objectionable book. In 1628 judges told the King that torture was not 'known or allowed in your land' and so should cease. It would have been interesting to ask the judges how they defined 'torture'.

SPOTLIGHT

SPOTLIGHT

MEAL TUB PLOT OF 1679–80

The queen of diamonds shows Mrs Cellier. She was a Catholic who employed an ex-prisoner to see if he could find out about any Protestant plot to offset the bad press the Catholics had had over the Popish Plot. Finding none, this man invented a plot and then arranged for its 'discovery'. Mrs Cellier's maid had hidden the details on a piece of paper under a meal tub, hence the name of the plot. But when it came out that the plot was a hoax, Mrs Cellier was pilloried in three different places. Although she wore armour under her clothes and held a bat, she was knocked down three times by stones, turnips and rotten eggs.

Quaker James Nayler having his tongue bored through for blasphemy in London in 1656

The pillorying of Mrs Cellier

CHAPTER 6

The Eighteenth Century

1. THE RELATIONSHIP BETWEEN CRIME AND SOCIAL STRESS

Before the eighteenth century, people had lived for generations in market towns and agricultural villages that changed little. Now they were faced with new lifestyles and problems in the unsettled society of the new industrial towns.

In some parts of the country the enclosure of land into compact farms, with isolated farmhouses, marked a change from the old open-field system and a central row of cottages. The poorest farm labourers lost their grazing rights and so had to depend solely on their wages. If the price of bread went up, the poor law system had to come to their aid. In 1723 the 'Black Act' was passed making it a felony to poach deer, fish or cut down trees with one's face blackened. This notorious act was repealed in 1827.

New industrial towns, centring on cotton mills or iron foundries, sprang up. Lancashire, once thinly populated, became the place to send unwanted paupers to as the mills cried out for labour. In 1787, St Clements Dane's parish, London, advertised in Manchester papers that it could supply pauper children in batches. These children found themselves working long hours, facing harsh punishments and sleeping in dormitory blocks.

Some parishes in Lancashire covered 100 square miles and their poor JPs and constables could not cope with the huge influx of people. Manchester's population in 1700 was 6,000 but by 1788 it had reached 50,000. Sheffield went from 2,695 in 1736 to 12,571 by 1755. In Merthyr Tydfil two JPs tried to cope with 30,000 people.

It was at this time that factory owners became JPs. But they lacked the traditional authority and feelings for community care of long-standing 'squire' families. Their whole way of life was based on exploiting their workers for profit. In their factories they were petty dictators, fining workers for swearing, smoking or being late. They could sack the troublesome and evict them from factory-built houses. So while the old parish officials with their limited powers could not cope in these new

towns, the industrialists could and did. Their methods, however, left
something to be desired.

The growth of turnpike roads and canals meant an increased sense of
mobility and thereby brought about further changes in the old way of life.
The Cotswolds and East Anglia ceased to be the main centres of
population. The North, the West and London expanded rapidly. Fewer
deaths, earlier marriages and more healthy births, easy-to-wash cotton
clothing and a more varied diet, all helped to increase the population from
5 million in 1700 to 6 million in 1750 and 9 million in 1801. The rich became
richer and the poor, poorer.

The landless farm workers and the rootless industrial workers were
confused and trapped by these changes. While some turned to Method-
ism to ease their miseries, others found escape in crime. The old moral
standards of the village could be forgotten in the backstreets of an
industrial town.

2.   THE FAILURE OF THE CRIME PREVENTION SYSTEM

Maintaining law and order depends on some form of policing. In the
eighteenth century high constables were middle-class people who
supervised the petty constables in their hundreds. They had to make sure
there were enough petty constables to keep order at executions and
whippings. They also distributed Sir John Fielding's *Hue and Cry* (see pp.
82–3) to them and in doing so helped bring about the new policing system
as we shall see. However, in some places high constables had become
little more than rate collectors. Petty constables were still appointed under
the Anglo-Saxon system of community policing.

Astonished citizens in the new industrial towns found themselves given
titles of tithingman or borsholder! They were expected to walk their areas
at least once every 24 hours and visit the alehouses once a week to report
any unlawful games or drunkenness. If a riot occurred they had to rush
along to the nearest JP with their staves to get their orders. They did this
for no pay and had to wait to the end of the year to get any expenses
repaid. In 1751 a petty constable of Sutton, Surrey, tried to serve a warrant
on a labourer's wife. She 'tore it into several pieces, some of which she put
into her mouth and chewed them and then spit it out on the ground and
immediately struck him . . . several times in the face'. Court records
continually listed assaults on constables, JPs and other officials. Almost all
prosecutions were still private ones. The victim got a constable from his
home to go with him to the JP to obtain a warrant.

By 1770 the old constable system had almost broken down. It was hampered by carrying out warrants and drawing up jury lists. But it was cheap to run and so the government continued it. The only national force that existed was the much-hated revenue officer force, which specialised in catching smugglers. As the large new industrial towns, such as Birmingham, Sheffield and Manchester, sprang up they were simply 'policed' by the old Anglo-Saxon constable system run by the overworked JPs.

True, there were poorly paid night watchmen too. Henry Fielding, the Bow Street JP (see pp. 77–81) said they were chosen 'out of those poor, old decrepit people who are for want of bodily strength rendered incapable of getting a livelihood by work'. Patrick Colquhoun, JP, said the 'old and infirm were thus employed so as to keep them out of the workhouse'. No wonder they were called 'Charleys'! They dated back to Charles II's reign. Matthew Wood, Lord Mayor of London, wrote:

> '. . . the beats or rounds of many *watchmen* are so short that they take only five minutes to walk them; which, being twice within the hour, he is either fifty minutes in his box, or what is more frequent, they meet two or three together, and are in conversation a considerable time; frequently they are employed in shutting up shops, or going on errands for the inhabitants, going into public houses with prostitutes; and although the streets are crowded with disorderly women, they will not interfere, or take the least notice of their conduct; also from the practice of their being fixed in stations or boxes for many years, there is no doubt but some of them receive bribes from persons who commit robberies in the streets as well as in houses; for it is a well known fact, that notorious characters attend Fleet Street and other public streets every night, and are in constant conversation with prostitutes, and must be well known to the watchmen.'

London and other large towns were also the victims of *trading JPs* who set up *justice shops*. They made a business of selling alehouse licences, arrest warrants, and arresting travellers and citizens out at night for the legal fees they could get from them. In fact they thrived on crime and so had no interest in suppressing it! Similarly *bum bailiffs* seized debtors and held them in *sponging houses* (small lock-ups), forcing them to pay highly for food and lodging. These bailiffs were hated by the public that felt they were wrongly treating people as 'criminals'. *Thief-takers* (see pp. 67–9) pocketed reward money for successful prosecutions of criminals no better than themselves. They sold 'Tyburn tickets' for up to 10 guineas which exempted buyers from duties such as acting as a constable. They had got these tickets when they helped convict a felon. William Payne was a London thief-taker and between 1768 and 1771 he prosecuted 69 people for theft, assault, riot, etc.. He used to mingle with crowds and look out for pickpockets. However, the underworld got its revenge on him by beating him up several times and twice setting on fire his carpenter's shop.

'Tom getting the best of a Charley', by Isaac and George Cruikshank, Life in London *(1820)*

A 'Charley' on his rounds

Q1   *Describe what is going on in the top picture. What is a 'Charley'?
Compare the 'hooligans' with those of today. Why are the 'Charleys'
powerless to deal with Tom and Jerry (the man standing behind Tom in
the picture)?*

Q2   *Why do you think the old man in the lower picture is a 'right Charley'?*

Community policing took on a new form as a result of eighteenth-century lawlessness. In most market towns associations designed to protect interests were started. Associations of florists to stop flower stealing and associations of farmers against horse stealing sprang up.

Some crimes like those connected with work came to be regarded by many as 'social crimes' rather than outright theft. Factory workers who took wood, metal or cloth, and farm labourers who poached, argued that these items were 'perks' that went with the job. On the other hand most classes regarded the majority of theft as anti-social and immoral.

As opposed to theft, offences against public order, such as minor assaults, swearing, gambling and drunkenness, were seen by the poor and many better class people as no worse than speeding offences today. Nevertheless, some crimes were direct challenges to authority, such as pulling down new hedgerows following land enclosure, smashing turnpike gates to avoid paying tolls.

3. JONATHAN WILD, 1683–1725, THIEF-TAKER GENERAL OF GREAT BRITAIN AND IRELAND

Born about 1683, Jonathan Wild was to get control of the underworld of London in the early eighteenth century. Without people grasping what he was up to he would organise a robbery and then help the victims to get their property back for which they rewarded him. He ran a Lost Property Office near the Old Bailey and Newgate Prison. Here he kept a list of stolen goods, while taking care to keep the actual goods in secret warehouses. This meant no-one could accuse him of having the goods himself. He also kept details on thieves. He put an 'X' against their names when he had enough evidence to hang them and a second 'X' when they were hanged. Could this be the origin of 'double-crossing' someone?

Jonathan Wild began his career as a thief-taker in 1713 when he became the unofficial 'deputy' to the corrupt Under-Marshal Hitchen. Wild took care that thieves only gave him details of their thefts and never brought the goods to him. To begin with, he would go to a victim's house and say he was sorry to hear of their loss in a recent robbery. He would add that he was an honest pawnbroker who had become suspicious of a recent consignment he had been offered, and thought perhaps it might contain goods stolen from the victim. If he was asked how he knew the goods were stolen and might belong to the victim, he said 'it was meerly Providential; being by meer Accident, at a Tavern, . . .' If the victim became suspicious he would leave, saying, 'Sir, I come only to serve you,

> **Q1** *What 'social crimes' are there today? Have people a right to disregard the law in this way?*

and if you think otherwise, I must let you know that you are mistaken. . . .' If the victim was too grateful to suspect a trick, he would arrange for the victim to meet the thieves at a street corner where the thieves would return the goods for cash. Later on, when he was famous, he would wait for victims to come to him in his office.

He also got gang members to charge each other with crimes until he had control of the gang or had wiped it out. He divided London up into operational areas for different gangs. He got some gangs to specialise in court or parliamentary robberies and others to strike at parties, fairs or churches. He recruited men to serve him either directly from prison or if they had returned from transportation to America before their time and were still 'on the run', he blackmailed them into serving him.

A joke invitation to Wild's execution

Q1 *What does 'Tripple Tree' refer to in the picture? Identify the objects in the small pictures.*

When Under-Marshal Hitchen realised Wild was making more of a profit than he was, he began a publicity campaign against thief-takers and a particular one whom he did not name at first. Wild replied by saying 'Thief-taker' should be seen as an honourable title, as he had had 60 executed and others transported. From then on he called himself 'Thief-taker General of Great Britain and Ireland' in the advertisements which proclaimed his services.

Wild had managed to combine running the underworld and 'policing' the city. His Lost Property Office depended both on a regular supply of stolen goods and the thanks of the victims. What the victims did not know was that their money helped finance fresh robberies. The more control Wild had on the thieves the more the public thanked him. He wiped out the gangs which he did not control, pinning 70 robberies and a murder on one gang alone. Soon he bought himself a coach and six horses and turned one of his rooms into a museum of rogues' items to impress his clients. Every morning robbers and lawyers queued up to see Wild in his bedroom to plead with him to help them as he breakfasted on a pint of sherry and a bowl of thick chocolate. Gradually he extended his operations over much of England. His private posse acted like a crime squad. When the Privy Council asked for his advice to check the growth in highway robberies, he suggested increasing the reward. In 1722 he bought a ship to export stolen items.

But time was running out for Wild. Other gangs began to seek their revenge, as Blueskin's attempt on Wild's life showed (see p. 71). Eventually he lost the sympathy of the public by his arrest of Jack Sheppard (see pp. 71-2). JPs gathered evidence against Wild. This frightened the City Recorder into arresting Wild rather than being accused of negligence himself. It was announced that Wild had formed a 'Kind of Corp of Thieves', had divided the country into gang areas, received stolen goods, put them in warehouses, pretended to be a government official and supplied false evidence. In the end he was found guilty of receiving ten guineas for helping to recover some lace, but failed to capture the criminals (whom he had ordered to carry out the crime in the first place). He was found guilty of this under a section of the 1719 Second Transportation Act, nicknamed 'The Jonathan Wild Act', which said anyone taking a reward for returning stolen goods and not arresting the thief and giving evidence against him was guilty of a felony.

In vain Wild pleaded for a royal pardon, displaying the wounds he had received over the years arresting criminals. By then he had survived two fractures of the skull (his bald head was covered with silver plates), seventeen wounds, and a cut throat. Both he and his wife failed in their suicide attempts and he was executed at Tyburn in 1725. His buried body was secretly dug up for a surgeon's use and the skin found a few days later. His skeleton is now in the Royal College of Surgeons' museum. So ended the life of the first modern gangster.

A thief distracting his victim before robbing him at Bartholomew Fair in 1739 (see p.58)

Q1   *Lay out a newspaper to mark Jonathan Wild's execution. Deal with (a) his career; (b) his execution; (c) an interview with Blueskin (see p.71) or a victim of Wild; (d) an interview with the Lord Mayor about what should be done in future to curb crime in the light of the scandal of Wild's Lost Property Office system.*

Q2   *Do a strip-cartoon on Wild's life.*

Q3   *What are 'protection rackets' and how do they operate? Are they inevitable?*

JACK SHEPPARD, 1702–24

This thin, fair-haired man with a stammer was to be more famous for his prison escapes than for his petty thieving, which only got him a few shillings. By training as a locksmith he learnt how to pick locks. When his dim-witted girlfriend, 'Edgworth Bess', was arrested for causing a disturbance, he rescued her from the local lock-up. He was an active gang robber from 1723 to 1724, until a colleague, 'Hell & Fury' Sykes, got him arrested to gain the reward money. Jack got out of the small prison's roof the first night and when later recaptured he was put in the New Prison. With the aid of tools smuggled in, he got out by making a hole in his cell wall and then climbed a 22-foot wall hauling heavy Bess up too.

This made him a hero to his fellow thieves. But Jonathan Wild reported Jack when he and fat, lazy Blueskin Blake stole cloth from Mr Kneebone's shop. Jack was chained up in Newgate after Wild frightened Bess into disclosing his hiding place. He was found guilty, but with some outside help from Bess and Polly Maggot he managed to cut away a cell bar, squeezed through and walked out of the prison! Wild promptly got Bess arrested and she was given purges to make her talk. However, she did not know where Jack was. Ten days later he was caught by a posse of horsemen and armed men in coaches on Finchley Common.

Back in Newgate, he seemed cheerful, and became the centre of publicity. He was quoted as saying 'a File is worth all the Bibles in the World'. Soon Wild caught Blueskin, but the robber nearly succeeded in cutting Wild's throat with a blunt penknife. The next night, Jack, though loaded down with chains, padlocks and bars, made his escape. He broke down six iron-barred doors, several of which were secured on the far side, without tools in total darkness. He got onto the roof of Newgate's Gate Tower. He then returned to his cell to get blankets to lower himself to a nearby house roof and from there to the ground. Probably he used his handcuffs and an iron bar he tore from a chimney, but even so it was an amazing feat.

He was free for 10 days, but then found drunk in a gin-shop. Over 300 lbs of irons were put on him. His cell was constantly crowded, especially with clergymen who came to save his soul ('Gingerbread Fellows' Jack called them). He had his portrait painted. He pleaded for his life on the grounds that he had turned King's Evidence against many criminals, but he shocked the judge when he claimed God had aided his escapes. The turnkeys charged visitors to see him and he was executed in front of 250,000 people. He kicked and thrashed about for fifteen minutes before he died.

When his body was cut down two parties fought for it, one his gang friends and the other a 'Sporting Gent's' toughies who wanted to try to revive him in a nearby room! His body was tossed round and in the end troops had to be called in to ensure its burial. Blueskin was executed the previous day and Bess was transported.

4. DICK TURPIN, 1706–39

Dick Turpin trained as a butcher. He began his criminal career by stocking his shop with stolen animals. When a farmer discovered this, Dick fled and joined the Essex Gang who went in for violent house-breaking. In 1735 five of the gang engaged in a robbery of a widow named Shelley at Loughton, and threatened to kill her if she did not say where her money was. Dick pointed at her burning fire and swore at her, 'God damn your blood, you old bitch, if you won't tell me I'll set your arse on the grate'. At this her son gave the hiding place away and the gang made the big haul it had come for.

Q1   *Write a ballad about the career of Jack Sheppard entitled 'Jack's Jape'.*

Q2   *Why do some criminals become popular heroes? Should they?*

After beating up three women in another robbery, two of the gang were caught and executed. Dick, however, escaped arrest by jumping out of a window. He turned highwayman, working with Tom King from a cave in Epping Forest. Dick shot dead one of two men trying to get the reward offered for his capture. In 1737 he shot at two people in a coach, but missed. As the intended victims had recognised him, he decided it was unsafe to stay in Essex. He went to Yorkshire where he called himself John Palmer and worked as a horsedealer. He was arrested after threatening to shoot a neighbour. He was hanged at York in 1739 in a new suit and followed by five poor men he had each paid a handsome sum to act as his mourners. He was credited with having made a famous ride to York. This ride was in fact done by a thief named Nevison. This man robbed a sailor in Kent and then rode 200 miles in sixteen hours, in an age when a coach took three days to make the same journey, in order to establish an alibi. The enterprising thief was identified, though, and hanged.

Despite the fame that highwaymen like Dick Turpin achieved in songs and stories, the highway robberies and gang crimes they committed were rare compared to petty theft and assaults that went on in that period.

Dick Turpin in the cave in Epping Forest from which he set out to rob anyone who passed along the roads below

SAMUEL LISTER, JP, TRACKS DOWN A FORGER, 1756

How was a criminal who moved from county to county ever caught in the days before detectives and computers? In 1756 a certain William Wilkins was detained in Bradford for failing to pay several inn bills. In his pockets were bills of exchange and a promissory note, adding up to £1,200. Could they have been forged? Who was he and where had he come from?

Samuel Lister, JP, decided to find out. Wilkins said he came from Painswick in Somerset, but Lister was unsure if Painswick was in Somerset or in Gloucestershire (its actual location). Lister did not know whom to write to in either county. It is easy to see that there was no system at that time for passing information about suspects round the country. (Can you say how it is done today?) Lister had to act quickly or he would have to release Wilkins for lack of evidence.

At last he got the names of four West Country people, but not JPs, and he wrote to them. He also put an advertisement in the *General Evening Post*, listing all he knew of Wilkins and asking for help. He got four letters in reply to this advertisement. William Griffiths, steward to Lord Chedworth, said Wilkins must be Edward Wilson who with others had 'carried on a very villanous Act of Forgery against me, and as they pretend by my Lord's Orders to me to Advance Money for his Lordship's use'. Griffiths said two of those concerned had already been arrested. He pointed out that 'Wilkins' was the son of a tenant of Lord Chedworth, and this was why 'Wilkins' had a paper on him signed by the nobleman. Griffiths described him as a 'jolly fattish full eyed well looking man about 5 foot 10 inches high about 30 years of age rather Pale face . . . Hair Brown and generally wears a Dark brown wig. . . '. In all he had defrauded people in Gloucestershire of £5,000.

So Lister got Wilson sent to Gloucester and there he was sentenced to death. But he was not executed immediately – he was reprieved for a year – and he sent a cheeky letter to Lister demanding the return of the forged bills! Lister had to pay a barrister to help him over this demand and he felt annoyed at the trouble and expense this put him to. But as he had not spent three months pursuing the matter Wilson would never have been convicted. Very few JPs were as conscientious as Lister, and until a national method of spreading information about criminals could be devised, many villains would get away with their crimes.

Q1   *Write out the kind of advertisement you think Lister put in the paper about 'Wilkins'.*

5. SMUGGLING

Smuggling is a crime created by law. Unless laws are made either forbidding the import or export of something, or putting a high duty on something, trade in such items is not illegal. Once such a law is made, and profit can be made from avoiding it, smuggling starts up. So the history of smuggling is centuries old. But its golden age was the eighteenth century.

Behind a smuggling venture is the Venturer or Investor, the unseen figure who puts up the money for the transport of the illegal goods, say brandy from France. He would be a wealthy person, a farmer or trader, who had £500 to spare. The captain he employed would have a ship which could cross the Channel to the south coast in eight hours. Such ships might have concealed compartments for the brandy casks or tow them along. If the ship were chased, the casks could be released and later recovered.

On the shore the Lander would be in charge of hiding and distributing the goods. He would get his men to signal the ship in with a lantern.

In Kent, Sussex and Dorset, Tub-carriers wearing farm labourers' white smocks for identification, worked for the Lander, carrying two $4\frac{1}{2}$ gallon tubs each, one on the back and one on the chest. Payment for one night's work was more than a week's wages for a workman. Batmen protected them with long poles or clubs. The goods might be concealed in taverns. The Old Ship Inn, Filey, had a hollow beam to conceal tobacco, while the Three Mariners, Scarborough, had four entrances including a tunnel to the harbour. It also had various concealed hiding places. Distribution was then made to shops, innkeepers and wealthy people.

Sussex 'spout lantern' used by smugglers to signal smuggling ships. It shone the light down the metal spout so that it could not be seen except from the sea.

Opposed to the smugglers were the Revenue men of the Customs and Excise Service. The coastline was divided into 33 areas, each with its Collector, Customer and Controller and beneath them five officials per port. Teams of Riding Officers were based every few miles with a supervisor for every six men. They had to ride along their sections to watch for smugglers and take the necessary action. But there were too few of them to cope with the smugglers' gangs of 100 strong.

When Captain Harry Carter from Cornwall took his smuggled cargo to South Wales, he went ashore first to fix up sales. But he was arrested as a suspected Irish pirate and held for twelve weeks. His powerful friends secured his release and he went on with his smuggling.

Small deliveries by smugglers could be made by concealing flasks in hollow 'Smugglers' Bibles'

The most notorious incident involved the Hawkhurst gang in Dorset. Shortly after landing a cargo of brandy, tea and rum, they had been discovered and chased. The Preventive men had seized two tons of tea and 39 casks of drink and put them in their Customs House at Poole. But 30 smugglers broke in and retrieved them. As they carried them away one of the smugglers gave a passing friend of his, Daniel Chater, a bag of tea. Later on the generous smuggler was arrested and the authorities heard that Chater had seen him on the day concerned. So Customs Officer William Galley was sent to escort Chater to Chichester, where the authorities expected he would give evidence against the smuggler. On the way the two stopped at the White Hart, in Rowland's Castle. The landlady alerted four smugglers, who arrived and got the pair half-drunk. Then they whipped them and tied them under horses' bellies and dragged them along. They buried Galley, possibly while he was still alive, and chained Chater up and disfigured him with a knife. Finally they flung him down a 10–metre dry well and stoned him. A £500 reward was offered for each murderer. Three were executed and the fourth died in prison.

'The Bloody and Inhuman Smugglers throwing down Stones on the expiring Body of Daniel Chater, whom they had flung into Lady Holt Well.'

6. THE BOW STREET SOLUTION TO THE POLICING PROBLEM – THE FIELDING BROTHERS

The problem of tracking down criminals who moved round a lot came to be tackled by two London JPs at their Bow Street court. Henry Fielding, a poor barrister and author of such famous novels as *Tom Jones* and *Joseph Andrews*, became the Bow Street JP in 1748. He found his predecessor had taken £700 a year in fees, so he cut this to £300. He even used that sum to pay his clerk, while living on a small salary himself. As he had no faith in petty constables or night watchmen, he recruited six men himself. He made a careful study of the causes of crime and criminals' habits which he later published. He drew attention to the large number of vagabonds living in lodging houses and buying incredibly cheap gin. In such places, he claimed, decent behaviour and health were impossible and poverty and misery bred crime. He described gangs 100 strong running organised crime. He argued that public executions were among the main causes of crime because they glorified the criminal:

> 'The day appointed by the law for the thief's shame [his execution] is the day of glory in his own opinion. His procession to Tyburn, and his last moments there, are all triumphant. . . The design of those who first appointed executions to be public was to add the punishment of shame to that of death; in order to make the example an object of greater terror. But experience has shewn us that the event is directly contrary to this intention. . .'

The 'idle 'prentice executed at Tyburn' is the title of this picture

Q1 *Read the comments on executions (above and on the next page) again and then hold a discussion on whether public executions were good or bad for (a) law and order, (b) moral education.*

Q2 *Look at the Tyburn picture and say whether you think Henry Fielding was right or not.*

Q3 *Who is in the cart with the prisoner? Why? What is the executioner's attitude to the day's work? Notice the woman selling a 'last dying speech'. What is called the 'triple tree' in this picture?*

A visitor from overseas who had witnessed an English execution confirmed Fielding's view:

> 'The English laugh at the delicacy of other nations, who make it such a mighty matter to be hanged; their extraordinary courage looks upon it as a trifle. He that is to be hanged first takes care to get himself shaved and handsomely dressed, either in mourning, or in the dress of a bridegroom. This done, he sets his friends at work to get him leave to be buried and to carry his coffin with him. When his suit of clothes, his gloves, hat, periwig, nosegay, coffin, flannel dress for his corpse are brought and prepared, the main point is taken care of, his mind is at peace, and then he thinks of his conscience.'

Dr Johnson, author and close observer of his age, disagreed with Fielding, however, and argued for keeping public executions:

> 'No sir, it would not be an improvement [to have executions in private]. They object that the old method draws together a number of spectators. If they did not draw the spectators they would not answer their purpose. The old method is most satisfactory to all parties; the public is gratified with a procession; the criminal is supported by it. Why should all this be swept away?'

Fielding kept careful records of the reports he received. He sent lists of stolen property to pawnbrokers, inn keepers and stable managers. He did much to break up London gangs before handing over to his half-brother, blind Sir John Fielding, who ran the Bow Street Office from 1754 to 1780.

To the P U B L I C

All Persons who shall for the Future suffer by Robbers, Burglars, &c. are desired immediately to bring, or send, the best Description they can of such Robbers, &c. with the Time and Place, and Circumstances of the Fact, to Henry Fielding, Esq; at his House in Bow-Street.

An advertisement put into the papers by Henry Fielding.
Why do you think Fielding put this advertisement in the papers? How did he expect it would help in the fight against crime?

It was said that Sir John could recognise 3,000 criminals by their voices and that they were unnerved by this unusual talent. In 1755, he published a *Plan for Preventing Robberies within Twenty Miles of London.* His plan was for people living on the outskirts of London to form clubs and pay a subscription. The money was to be used to provide fast riders called Bow Street Runners to alert everyone along the route as they raced to Bow

Street with news of a crime. The success of the plan depended on the speed with which the public notified the Bow Street Runners that a crime had been committed. But the plan was probably never carried out. However, the bills he sent to the government in 1756 show that he had been busy: 'For dragging the ponds to find the clothes of Cannicot's wife that was murdered, £2 2s. [£2.10].' 'For opening a pavement on suspicion of murder, 12s. [60p].'

Henry Fielding

Sir John produced another plan which was for six salaried JPs to supervise new police stations; strong guards on the main roads entering London; and a regiment of Light Horse to hand. The government rejected the regiment idea but gave him £600 to establish a civilian Horse Patrol of eight (later ten) men in 1763. These proved highly successful and by 1764 the roads were clear. The government promptly disbanded the Patrol. Back came the highwaymen within a few weeks. The Patrol was restarted; the highwaymen vanished; the Patrol was stopped; back came the highwaymen. But there was no Patrol again until 1805 because it was considered too expensive!

In 1805, 54 men were recruited and issued with blue coats and trousers, black boots and tall black leather hats, white gloves and scarlet waistcoats; hence their nickname of 'Robin Redbreasts'. Each carried a pistol, cutlass and truncheon. They had to be at least 5 feet 5 inches (about 1.65 m) tall.

Sir John's other notable contribution to the fight against crime was to make Bow Street into a crime information centre, with reports flowing in and publicity flowing out. His 1772 *General Preventative Plan* was the first plan to call for the collection, collation and circulation of information about criminals on a national scale. Sir John began by calling on JPs and mayors to supply him with details about crimes and suspects, and asking gaolers to keep descriptions of anyone brought into their prisons. In this way he extended what his half-brother Henry Fielding had done for London to the whole country. But, more important, he pieced together the information he received on various criminals so a complete description of them and their crimes could be circulated on posters. He started by printing his reports on the front page of each Monday's edition of the *London Packet or New Lloyd's Evening Post*, and then asked mayors and JPs to put it up prominently in towns throughout the country. Then every half year he issued lists of offenders still at large. He pressed JPs to make parish constables search for wanted criminals on his lists.

Sir John Fielding

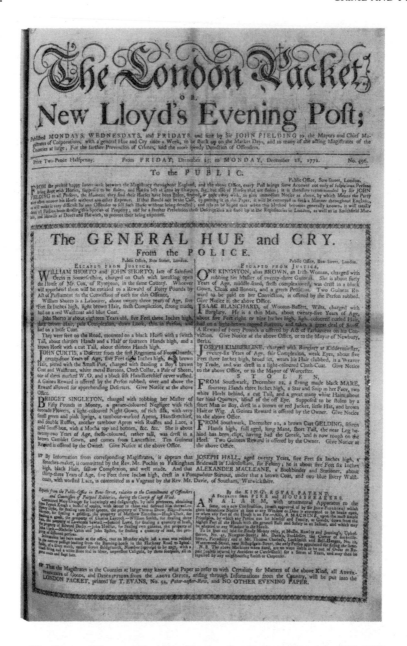

'The General Hue and Cry' *from* The London Packet *of December 28th 1772*

Q1 *Which day of the week are mayors and JPs advised to put this sheet on display? Why do you think Fielding recommended that day?*

Q2 *Draw a picture of one of the suspects and write underneath a description of him/her and what he/she had done.*

Did Sir John's *General Preventative Plan* work? Here is a typical example of its effectiveness. In July 1773 Richard alias John Myett, alias Early, alias Dart, alias Mason, stole silver from a silversmith's shop in Wallingford, Berks. Details were put in *The General Hue and Cry*. A fortnight later he was caught 130 miles away, but he escaped. He then burgled his former employers at Salisbury in February, 1774, and following a further advertisement he was caught 260 miles from Salisbury. He was hanged.

It is generally agreed that the plan was a success because it set up a 'policing' system without the need for new officials by simply using local JPs and existing law officers. In doing so, it avoided the centralised, State-controlled systems found in Europe, which were felt by Britons to challenge local liberties.

Later Sir John's sheet was called *The Hue and Cry and Police Gazette* and it is still published today. By 1775 Sir John had realised that in some country districts there were not enough JPs to operate the scheme and so he called for high constables to be based on the main roads within 100 miles of London and to be paid by their counties. Their houses were to be marked 'HIGH CONSTABLE'. But only three counties were willing to become involved in the plan. The rest said that their high constables had enough work to do already and were of too high a social status to be ordered to buy houses along main roads!

John Townsend, a typical Bow Street Runner

7. RIOTS AND THE MOB

Dealing with individual criminals was one thing, but what happened if mobs ran riot? Farm workers had already rebelled against the revolutionary changes of enclosure. Now new factory towns brought people closely together, and they could rebel against their employers.

The JPs' first line of defence was their constables operating as they had since Anglo-Saxon times (see Statute of Winchester, p. 19). But the constable system broke down in the eighteenth century as people bought their way out of their rota turn and useless watchmen replaced them. The JPs' second line of defence was the militia. In 1757 compulsory service by ballot was introduced and a *quota* (fixed number) of 18 to 45-year-olds was set for each county. However, it was possible to pay money to avoid doing your duty. And as these militiamen were local people they tended to side with their rioting neighbours. Worse, they were often untrained and it was difficult to muster them quickly in an emergency. These drawbacks meant that JPs were forced to rely more and more on the army.

Thus 'policing' of new industrial towns came to be done by troops. By the end of the eighteenth century forty barracks had been built in towns capable of holding a total of 20,000 troops. Once Norman castles had housed those responsible for subduing people; now army barracks served that purpose.

Norwich Barracks, 1793; token issued by John Rooks, timber merchant. The dragoon is surmounted by a motto which translates, 'For King and Country'.

In 1793 Prime Minister Pitt told the Commons, 'A spirit had appeared in some of the manufacturing towns which made it necessary that troops

> **Q1**   *See if a barracks was built in your nearest town about this time. If one was, find out if troops in it were used for riot control.*

should be kept near them'. By then parts of the North and Midlands resembled a country under military occupation as workers began to clamour for voting rights and better conditions. But the army could not be everywhere. Pitt encouraged community leaders to start volunteer corps which the government would arm. Some of the founders of these corps were encouraged by the thought of being called 'captain', 'major', and designing fanciful uniforms, drawing up their own rules and holding parades. But because these volunteer corps were essentially upper and middle class organisations, they were to provoke 'class warfare' in due course as the Peterloo Massacre of 1819 was to show (see pp.117–8).

Because troops were under Crown orders, JPs had to get War Office permission to use them. This often meant troops were not available until long after they were needed. To prevent delays, the War Secretary was allowed to issue orders in case the troops were needed. In 1766 he wrote to the commanding officers of the dragoons at Manchester and Warwick on hearing that JPs could not keep order:

> 'I have therefore unasked, but not uninformed of the present state of your Neighbourhood, sent you an Order . . . which I desire you will keep entirely to yourself till the Civil Magistrate shall apply to you for Assistance. If that never happens the Order had better never be known'.

In time, there was no need for secrecy. Standing orders were issued to troops to aid JPs when they called on them. Some saw this as a sinister development. In fact eighteenth-century lawyers did all they could to ensure that troops were seen as civilians in uniform under civilian and not military law. All citizens were required to help put down a riot, and this is what the troops were doing. But the use of armed civilians for policing raised thorny legal problems. For example, how much force could the troops use? If they did not use enough they might as troops be court-martialled, but if they used too much they might as civilians be charged with murder or manslaughter. Legal experts asked, too, what would happen if a court decided afterwards that an officer had been wrong in giving the order to fire?

Now let us see what happened when riots did occur.

Q1 *Answer the following questions:*
(a) Should policing be based on class structure? (b) Will the propertied class always suppress the working class if policing is based on class structure? (c) What alternative is there to class-structure policing? Remember that people thought highly of their liberties and did not want a European-style, government-controlled police force with spies.

Q2 *Why do you think the War Secretary added the last sentence in the quotation above?*

1. PORTEOUS RIOTS, 1737

New and severe rioting followed the hanging of a smuggler in Edinburgh. At the execution service, the smuggler's popular accomplice had tried to escape but his attempt had been foiled by troops. The crowds displayed sympathy for the accomplice. The locally hated Captain Porteous ordered his reluctant troops to fire when the crowd threw stones. Seventeen were killed or wounded. Porteous was sentenced to death for murder. When he appealed, the mob broke into the gaol and lynched him, hanging him from a home-made gibbet. The JPs and troops were too scared to stop them. Parliament stepped in and dismissed the provost (mayor) and made the city pay Porteous' widow £2,000.

2. GORDON RIOTS, 1780, LORD MAYOR KENNETT FINED £1,000 FOR CRIMINAL NEGLIGENCE FOR FAILING TO TAKE ACTION

The Gordon Riots, London 1780. The sack of Lord Doscat's house in Bloomsbury Square.

Q1 *Charles Fox said he would 'much rather be governed by a mob than by a standing army'. What did he mean and do you agree with him?*

Q2 *How would a riot be controlled today? Who would be responsible for doing what and why?*

Led by the crazy 30-year-old Lord George Gordon, a mob of 60,000 roughed up peers and MPs and demanded 'No Popery'. For the rest of the week they smashed up Catholic property in London. Though platoons of soldiers marched round, no JP was brave enough to give them orders. Neither would the officers use their own initiative, remembering Captain Porteous' fate. Sir John Fielding and another JP who tried to do something had their houses wrecked. Hatred against all authority soon motivated the mob and they released 300 prisoners from Newgate. Only when 300 troops stood watching the destruction of the Lord Chief Justice's house did a JP appear, read the Riot Act, and order the troops to fire. Five rioters were killed, but this only caused a temporary lull. Soon 15,000 soldiers were rushed to London, but no one knew what to do with them as the JPs remained in hiding.

To break the stalemate George III told the Privy Council that the officers of the troops must be allowed to decide when to fire. Some people wondered whether he was declaring martial law (military rule) to protect the property of the well-off. While coach drivers charged terrified citizens sky-high fares to flee from the mob, and rioters used a fire engine to pump a distillery's gin into the street to provide free drinks, John Wilkes took command of the troops defending the Bank of England! Gradually things quietened down. Gordon was found not guilty of high treason but the Lord Mayor was fined £1,000 for not putting a stop to the riot. The trial highlighted the mistaken belief that the Riot Act forbad the troops to fire until one hour after its reading. In all, 210 were killed, 75 died later, 405 were arrested, and 25 were hanged.

During the following weeks pamphlets deploring the use of troops for riot control were published. They called for a revival of the *posse comitatus*, a reorganised militia and tougher laws. But the institution of a full-scale police force was clearly disliked. Voluntary associations to defend property sprang up everywhere, even though there was a general feeling that such riots would never occur again. When Pitt introduced a Police Bill for London in 1785, he was forced to withdraw it as unnecessary. Opponents said the 1414 act of Henry V requiring every citizen to help suppress riots would still apply in an emergency.

8. REFORM OR REVOLUTION

The 1790s saw a growing demand for a reform of the corrupt and unfair parliamentary election system. Unfortunately the French Revolution suggested to many that any reform would trigger off a revolution. When the French revolutionaries offered to help other lands to overthrow their kings and nobles their worst fears seemed to be confirmed. The London Corresponding Society (LCS) which linked intelligent craftsmen of the big industrial towns together began to hold huge open-air demonstrations

in 1794. Prime Minister Pitt acted ruthlessly, arresting the ringleaders. Shortly after its appointment a Commons' Committee of Secrecy reported that it had found evidence of the workers being armed. Actually its evidence was very weak. As the King went down to Parliament, printer Kid Wake shouted out, 'No George, no war!' He was picked out of the crowd and sentenced to five years' solitary imprisonment. He served this at Gloucester Prison. Its individual cell system (see pp. 100–3) made it an ideal place to isolate political activists even from fellow prisoners.

KIDD WAKE,

IN A SOLITARY CELL,

AND CLOATHED IN THE UNIFORM OF GLOCESTER PENITENTIARY HOUSE.

Kid Wake in his yellow-blue uniform in his cell. This poster was produced by him after his release. He was well treated, not kept in isolation and only had stomach upsets after visits from his wife!

Soon Thomas Hardy, shoemaker and president of the LCS, the Revd. Horne Tooke and ten others were on trial for treason. The government had very carefully selected the jury from wealthy citizens like Matthew Whiting, a sugar refinery owner. But the jury acquitted the defendants within six minutes after hearing the defence lawyers argue that the prisoners had done no treasonable deed. For the government to claim that anyone who criticised how they ran the country was a traitor would mean no one would be able to say anything against a government again!

One newspaper called it 'the most important crisis in the history of English liberty, that the world ever saw'. Erskine for the defence, called on the court to 'distinguish between an intention to kill the king and an intention to reform the House of Commons'. The crowd outside the court carried the jury off to a slap-up meal and commemorative medals and tokens were struck to mark the event.

The Horne Tooke trial token; Erskine and Gibbs were the defence lawyers; the twelve names are those of the jury, including the present author's ancestor, Matthew Whiting

A furious government was left with 800 arrest warrants which it had intended to use once the leaders had been found guilty. The unused warrants are still in the Public Record Office.

The severe winter of 1794–5 and the bread riots at Tewkesbury and the Forest of Dean in July 1795 reminded people that the misery of cold weather and food shortages had sparked off the French Revolution. When Hardy retired the LCS elected a 22-year-old Irish plumber, John Binns, to lead them. Binns had said he was prepared to use violence and he had his connections with the United Irishmen and the French. Huge orderly meetings followed. In October, at Copenhagen Fields on the outskirts of London, 100,000 people heard speakers describe the starvation some faced in a land of plenty for others. Unpoliced London was alarmed. Three days later something struck the King's coach and he arrived at the House of Lords, stammering, 'My Lords, I, I, I've been shot at!' The next day 300 troops and 500 constables guarded his visit to Covent Garden and the wealthy audience sang the National Anthem six times over.

Quickly Pitt saw to the passing of the Act against Treasonable Practices, making it treason to speak or write against the British system of

---

Q1 *Do you believe 'British justice' had been done as the Horne Tooke trial token claims?*

government, and the Act against Seditious Meetings, by which no meetings of over 50 persons were allowed without a JP's permission. Two days later 200,000 LCS supporters gathered at Copenhagen Fields again to make a mockery of that act! It was clear that it would take an army to stop such meetings.

In 1796 and early 1797 three attempts by the French to invade Britain and aid the British workers failed disastrously. Late in 1797 naval mutinies took place. At the Nore in the Thames Estuary Richard Parker, an expelled naval officer who had been sent back into the lower ranks, stirred the mutineers up with his LCS ideas. He called on them to sail the fleet up the river to bombard the Tower of London – England's Bastille. The government was so worried that it lit the furnaces of the Thames forts to heat the cannon balls to fire at its own ships! However, a kind of SAS recapture of the ships was brought off and Parker hung from the rigging of his ship. The Incitement to Mutiny Act was quickly passed, making it a capital felony to encourage the forces to revolt. This act was to be used against the Tolpuddle Martyrs in 1834 and the Communists in the 1920s.

In 1799 Binns and two others were sentenced to three years in Gloucester Prison. It was notable that the reform system in use there (see pp. 97–103) completely changed Binns and he ended his life as a distinguished American citizen. A marked increase in the number of volunteer corps occurred at this time as propertied people prepared against invasion and insurrection. In 1799 and 1800 Pitt's Combination Acts forbad all political societies. In vain Fox said, 'I know that liberty is the greatest blessing that mankind can enjoy and peace the next'. Pitt's measures crushed the radical movements until the war against Napoleon was over, but in the end they were to burst forth again.

9. THE HULKS AND TRANSPORTATION, EIGHTEENTH AND NINETEENTH CENTURIES

In 1678 Parliament approved the idea of sending prisoners to serve their sentences in the American colonies of Virginia and Maryland and in the West Indies where they could be of use in those developing lands. An act

---

Q1 *Would the prisoners tried for treason in 1794 have been found guilty if they had been charged a few years later under the Treasonable Practices Act? If so, why?*

Q2 *Answer the following questions: (a) Do you think Parliament has a right to pass laws like those of 1795 and 1799? When and why? (b) Would it be true to say only the verdict of a jury stood between liberty and tyranny under these laws? Who would then represent 'the people', Parliament or the jury?*

of 1717 ruled that those convicted of certain 'benefit of clergy' felonies could be transported for seven years and certain non-clergyable felonies for fourteen years.

Firms such as *Messrs Stephenson & Randolf, felon dealers, Bristol,* sprang up to handle the shipments, making their profit by selling the convicts on their arrival. In 1740 a convict could fetch up to £80 in the West Indies. Many acts were passed in the eighteenth century making transportation the punishment for more and more offences. Between 1717 and 1776, 30,000 were transported. But when the Americans declared their independence in 1776 a crisis arose because British prisons could not cope with the overcrowding caused by the sudden end of transportation to America. At that time 960 a year were sent there. This crisis was to continue for some years and become a major factor in the prison reform movement (see p. 97). Indeed, the crisis ceased only when the possibilities of Australia as an alternative 'dumping ground' were realised.

Prison hulk York *receives a new batch of prisoners*

In the meantime disused ships, *hulks,* were used as emergency prison accommodation. Between August 1776 and March 1778, a quarter of the prisoners put on these hulks died from the unsanitary conditions aboard.

Some improvements were made after an inquiry, but in the early nineteenth century, as a hulk chaplain reported, the hot summer nights made:

> 'the heat between decks so oppressive as to make the stench intolerable, and to cause the miserable inmates frequently to strip off every vestige of clothing and gasp at the port-holes for a breath of air'.

The convicts' work consisted of cleaning the outsides of ships, stacking timber, cleaning guns and particularly dredging channels in the Thames. They worked in gangs of ten to twenty.

In 1787 a convoy of ships left Portsmouth with 736 convicts (including 200 females) for Australia. Jeremy Bentham (see p.138) imagined a judge might have said to them:

> 'I sentence you, but to what I know not; perhaps to storm and shipwreck, perhaps to infectious disorders, perhaps to famine, perhaps to be massacred by savages, perhaps to be devoured by wild beasts. Away – take your chance; perish or prosper, suffer or enjoy; I rid myself of the sight of you'.

It is certain that over 40 of the 736 died on the voyage.

Compulsory bath on board the convict ship HMS Success. *Prisoners were pushed into the tank, the grating was closed and a warder scrubbed them with a long broom.*

Q1   *Do you think Bentham's comment on sentencing convicts to transportation to Australia was fair?*

From the government's point of view, transportation had advantages and disadvantages. On the plus side, the prisoners would be far enough away not to be a problem and they could open up possible trade with China and the Pacific Islands. On the minus side, the distant settlement meant each convict cost far more a year to look after than those in prisons at home.

The convicts' destination, Botany Bay, was too barren for settlement, so in fact they were taken on to Port Jackson. But life was harsh there too. In 1790, as no ship had called for 32 months, supplies were so low that half the convicts had to be moved to Norfolk Island to survive. When ships did arrive later that year they brought 750 more convicts (250 had died on the voyage) of whom 500 were sick. In 1791, 1,864 more arrived. Those who were sent to work for settlers lived reasonably well, while those in the barracks suffered badly from brutal treatment. Eventually a *ticket-of-leave* system for good behaviour was introduced.

Things improved under Governor Macquarie who arrived in 1809. He had better quarters built and gave good convicts land to develop. When John Bigge arrived in 1819 to investigate the situation for the government, he was astonished that 'Botany Bay' was no longer a gaol, but a healthy colony relying on convict labour, and where the convicts did not live in terror as he thought they should do. It bothered him that they also had good food and quarters. He suggested harder work and stricter control, as well as sending more of them into the wilderness to open up the sheep farming.

The 1830s saw the beginning of the Assignment System. Under it, government officials at the point of destination picked out skilled convicts (for example, carpenters) and kept them in barracks, while the rest were 'assigned' to free settlers. The Assignment Board met twice a week to receive applications for convicts and to decide who should be sent where. Employers had to pay male convicts £10 a year and female ones £2, but for the convict everything depended on how the employer would treat him or her. The Tolpuddle Martyrs, sentenced in 1834 for forming a secret-society trades union, were given a blanket, some raw beef and flour and told to tramp to their farms. James Hammett slept under trees at night, stripping the bark off for shelter. Tom Standish had to walk 150 miles to his farm.

In due course one could get a ticket-of-leave (after four years of a seven-year sentence), then a *conditional pardon* (one or two years later) and finally an absolute pardon, or *certificate of freedom,* if one had served one's full term. Many ticket-of-leave men became constables, overseers of chain-gangs, or shopkeepers. They had to report twice a year and stay in the vicinity. Those with pardons were called *emancipists* ('emancipated' means set free by mercy) while those who had completed their sentences were *expirees.* Conditional pardons, unlike absolute pardons, did not include the right to return to Britain.

Fierce dogs were used to ensure that convicts did not escape from the peninsula linking Port Arthur to Van Diemen's Land

In 1826 Sydney Smith pointed out to Home Secretary Peel that men sentenced to be transported were relieved of having to care for their families, exchanged a bad climate for a fine one, and gained the prospect of future prosperity for no work! Indeed many ex-convicts made good in the new land. In 1838 the Molesworth Committee on Transportation said transportation was not a sufficient punishment. Convicts were treated unequally. Transportation lacked terror even though 50 to 100 lashes were given as punishments. The Committee also said transportation was very expensive. The Committee concluded that between 1787 and 1836 the 75,200 convicts sent there had cost the government £8 million, and that the convicts were hardened, not reformed, by their experience. The Committee wanted transportation halted and replaced by two to fifteen years hard labour at home. But 4,000 a year continued to be transported. In 1839 Lord Russell, Home Secretary, said it meant 'Crime is not punished as crime . . . The question of colonial profit and loss mixes with the award of justice. A man is estimated by his capacity as a colonist, not by his crime as a felon.'

Q1 *Put Lord Russell's comment into your own words. What is your opinion of what he said?*

In 1842 the Probation System replaced the Assignment System. Those transported for life had to start their sentences on the harsh Norfolk Island. Other male convicts spent one to two years in graded probation gangs doing hard labour. On completing probation, a prisoner could become a *pass-holder*. He progressed next through three classes of pass-holder to complete half his sentence before getting first a ticket-of-leave and then a pardon or free certificate. Pass-holders could earn money. The system was a severe one and it was not very satisfactory. Women served their probationary period in a 'female penitentiary' on the hulk *Anson* at Hobart, which held 519. They spent their time sewing shirts, dresses, etc.

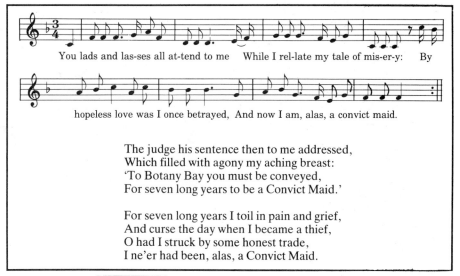

You lads and las-ses all at-tend to me While I rel-late my tale of mis-er-y: By

hopeless love was I once betrayed, And now I am, alas, a convict maid.

> The judge his sentence then to me addressed,
> Which filled with agony my aching breast:
> 'To Botany Bay you must be conveyed,
> For seven long years to be a Convict Maid.'
>
> For seven long years I toil in pain and grief,
> And curse the day when I became a thief,
> O had I struck by some honest trade,
> I ne'er had been, alas, a Convict Maid.

Words and music to The Convict Maid

10. EIGHTEENTH-CENTURY PRISONS: JOHN HOWARD, SIR GEORGE O. PAUL AND WILLIAM BLACKBURN

John Howard, 1726–90, was literally to give his life for the cause he fought for when he died of gaol fever (typhus) in Russia. He was there inspecting prisons in the cause of prison reform. This son of a wealthy Hackney upholsterer first saw the inside of a prison when taken prisoner-of-war by the French in 1756. But it was not until he became high sheriff of Bedford in 1773 that he began his self-imposed task of inspecting every prison in Britain and Europe. His inherited wealth enabled him to spend years on this task. Today, this would need a government or a charity to find an academic team and offer opportunities of Ph.D. degrees for those taking part. In all, he travelled 80,000 km during his tour of inspection.

Equipped with a measuring tape and a pair of scales to weigh food rations, he visited first county gaols and then the small town lock-ups and houses of correction. When the Revd. John Wesley, another endless traveller, met him in Dublin, he noted:

> 'I had the pleasure of a conversation with Mr Howard, I think one of the greatest men in Europe. Nothing but the mighty power of God can enable him to go through his difficult and dangerous employments. But what can hurt us, if God is on our side?'

The Christian mission of Wesley and others made people ready to listen to Howard's findings when they were published as *The State of the Prisons in England and Wales* in 1777.

The condemned hold in Newgate

Imagine Howard riding up to a prison, asking the gaoler to be allowed to look round. Out would come his tape measure and notebook. Every room would be measured and the state of its floor, walls, airiness and light noted down. Was there anywhere for exercise? Were the prisoners segregated or did the sexes intermingle and have children? What was the food ration? Was any religious instruction or medical care provided? How many died of illness each year? How was the gaoler paid?

He found some gaols had no sewers while others, like Knaresborough, had open sewers running right through them. His own clothes stank so much after such visits that he could not travel in a coach. He tabulated his findings, placing great emphasis on exact details. He pointed out that a

Q1 *Who is the figure standing in the centre of the picture? Why is he there?*

Q2 *How are the prisoners secured? What furniture is there?*

prisoner's moral behaviour was worsened, not improved, by such conditions. He highlighted the fact that diseased prisoners spread their diseases to judges and juries and caused epidemics in their home towns when released. As 1,000 prisoners a year died from disease a prison sentence was virtually a death sentence by lottery. In Gloucester gaol, three times as many died of fever as were hanged. He also made it clear that there was no point in running such prisons other than to detain troublemakers:

> 'In some Gaols you see . . . boys of twelve and fourteen eagerly listening to the stories told by . . . experienced criminals, of their adventures, successes, stratagems and escapades.'

Prisoners gambled and drank heavily, a situation positively encouraged by gaolers who made their profit by selling drink to them. If there was a policy of trying to improve prisoners' behaviour or help them solve their difficulties, there would have to be staff trained for such a task. Could a prison be designed to reform as well as detain? Those were the pressing questions which Howard's inquiry raised. His book contained much advice on what should be done too. But how could one turn a broken down old fever-ridden building run by a grasping gaoler for his own profit into a healthy reforming establishment manned by trained staff? In short, how could conditions in prisons be improved? Two factors led to the changes in prison conditions throughout Britain. First, and most important, there was the danger of a serious outbreak of gaol fever in Britain. Second, the outbreak of the American War of Independence had stopped transportation to the colonies and so increased the prison population in Britain by 84 per cent almost overnight.

Such overcrowding dramatically increased the incidence of gaol fever (typhus) which is transmitted by lice, although people in those days thought it was caused by bad air. Sir George O. Paul (1746–1820), who was to lead the Gloucestershire reform movement, wrote *Thoughts on the Alarming Progress of Gaol Fever* in 1784. In his book, he argued that no sentence should condemn a prisoner to death by disease or hunger. He said the symptoms were 'low fever, attended by a violent thirst, and heat of the skin . . . with a disorder in the head'. Individuals should push lint dipped in camphorated vinegar up their noses, while places should be fumigated with sulphur or tobacco. The real solution was an airy prison. But could such a prison be a secure one? Certainly it must be purpose-built, and that would require an architect who could grasp what was needed for such a new type of architecture.

Sir George O. Paul was the ideal man to respond to Howard's call for action. A wealthy clothier, he had idled his life away until appointed county high sheriff of Gloucestershire in 1780. From then on he was to

Q1 *Why would the boys listen so eagerly? What is meant by 'stratagems'?*

*Bust of Sir George O. Paul,
Gloucestershire prison
reformer, on his tomb in
Gloucester Cathedral*

devise a reform system and see to the construction of the county gaol and four houses of correction in the county. He got the local gentry and clergy involved in the task and badgered Parliament into passing the Gloucester-shire Act, 1785, empowering them to buy land, build the prisons, draw up rules and employ trained staff.

William Blackburn (1750–90) was to become internationally known for the prisons he designed for Sir George O. Paul. In the end his designs were used in the building of half the new prisons in England. He had to ensure they fulfilled three requirements: (1) security; (2) healthiness; (3) separa-tion of prisoners.

1. SECURITY

A strong perimeter wall, 5.4m high, provided security while allowing freedom for exercise within it. Buttress supports were put on the outside to prevent inmates scaling them and large stones were used so they could not be eased out. *Chevaux de frize* – iron spikes on a rod which spun round when gripped – were installed on top of the wall. The buildings were arranged so that the staff could see what was going on. His Northleach House of Correction's polygonal (many-sided) radial design was to be copied in England and the USA.

A Summary of John Howard's Report on Gloucestershire County Gaol in Gloucester Castle, 1777

Gaoler was William Williams; he got no salary but could charge fees from the prisoners who were committed to his care; he could sell beer to them. The debtors got no food allowance but felons got 'six-penny loaf in two days'. Garnish was 1s 6d. This meant that newcomers had to pay this sum for the entertainment of all. Chaplain was Revd. Mr Evans and he took three services a week and was paid £40 a year. No surgeon, but one could be applied for.

'[There was] only one court for all prisoners; and one small day room, 12 ft by 11 [3.6 m by 3.35 m], for men and women felons. The free ward for debtors is 19 ft by 11 [5.79 m by 3.35 m], which having no window, part of the plaster wall is broke down for light and air. The night-room for men-felons, though up many stone steps, is close and dark; and the floor is so ruinous, that it cannot be washed. The whole prison is out of repair. Many prisoners died here in 1773 . . . eight died about Christmas 1778 of the small pox. No infirmary . . . There is no proper separation of the women. The licentious intercourse of the sexes is shocking to decency and humanity. Five or six children have lately been born in this gaol. There is a chapel, but all the endeavours of the chaplain to promote reformation among the prisoners must necessarily be defeated, by the inattention of the magistrates, and their neglect of framing and enforcing good regulations.'

---

2. HEALTH

The gatehouse contained a *lazaretto*, or isolation section for new arrivals. (The name derives from Lazarus in St John's and St Luke's Gospels.) Howard had examined lazarettos in Mediterranean sea-ports. In the lazaretto they had a much needed bath, their clothes were fumigated and they received a health check before being allowed to go on to their cell block.

The perimeter wall was set well clear of the buildings to allow air to circulate, while the buildings themselves were designed to draw fresh air in through their piazza arch design and then let it out through ventilation chimneys. Outside balconies giving access to cells reduced the need to use airless corridors. Circular iron gratings in floors and 'portcullis'-style iron doors aided airflow, as did the use of iron-frame bedsteads instead of plank beds.

Each prisoner had a centrally heated day cell (2.3 m x 1.7 m) and an unheated night cell to himself. A bath was supplied to each block. The exercise yards were separated by 4.8 m-high palisades to allow air circulation.

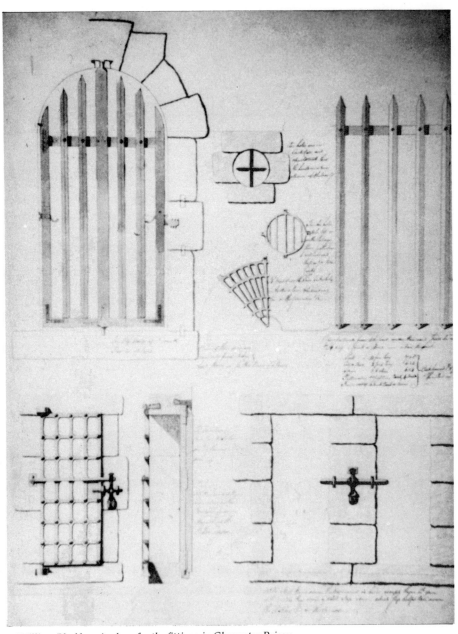

William Blackburn's plans for the fittings in Gloucester Prison

3. THE SEPARATION OF PRISONERS

The prison was divided into the Gaol for those awaiting trial and the Penitentiary (place for doing penance) for those serving sentences. These two sections were subdivided into male and female parts. A chapel was provided for encouragement, workrooms for the discipline of hard labour and darkened cells for punishment.

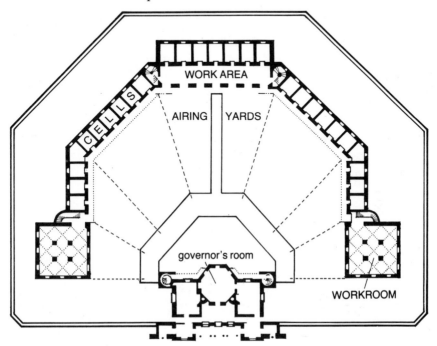

Ground Plan for Northleach House of Correction, designed by William Blackburn, 1785

4. PAUL'S SEPARATE SYSTEM

In Sir George Paul's time, as in ours, the question was asked: is it possible to reform prisoners at all? The answer, then as now, depended on what you believed about human nature. In the eighteenth century it was felt that human nature was neutral and could be influenced by good or bad. Just as gaol fever was said to be transmitted by bad air, so moral health was affected by invisible substances passing from person to person. One's surrounding, it was thought, was all important; if you could change a person's environment, you could alter that person's character.

Immoral behaviour was due to bawdy entertainment and passion. Places of low entertainment attracted criminal types; going to such places was

Q1 *Can you say how the design of Northleach House of Correction aids security and airflow?*

likely to contaminate the visitor. Howard had been shocked to find billiards, tennis, skittles and drink parties flourishing in the Fleet Prison! In the eighteenth century 'passion' meant desires such as greed, hatred and violence. It was the opposite of 'sentiment', which included reasonableness and gentleness. Criminals had given in to passions and so in a sense were madmen. One's environment brought out either one's passions or one's sentiments.

The cure for criminal behaviour, said Paul, was *solitude*. Because a person is corrupted by bad company he can be freed from 'passion' if he is deprived of company for a period. If his only contacts in the purpose-built prison are with the staff, the isolation of solitude will make him pause to think and then respond to the opportunities of renewed health, education, work, and religious instruction. Sir George Paul realised care had to be taken not to let a prisoner become too isolated in case he became suicidal. Regular work and religious instruction were to balance the solitude and as time went on the prisoner was to be allowed more and more contact with his fellow prisoners.

View of the new county gaol, Gloucester

Q1 *Examine the picture above carefully. List the security features and the health features which the architect has planned. How has separation been achieved? This prison is still in use, although much changed. Today three prisoners have one cell, instead of each prisoner having two cells.*

William Blackburn understood what Sir George Paul was getting at and provided him with buildings designed to make such reform work possible. But buildings alone are not enough; a daily system of running the life within them is essential. Rules were needed if Sir George Paul's three points of security, health and separation were to be achieved. He devised a rule book that was so good that other prison authorities based their systems on it. In his Rule Book, he laid down rules for the staff as well as the prisoners. The key to good staff work, he argued, was the journal or record book. The governor had to record any problems that arose and any actions he took each day, while the surgeon and the chaplain had similar journals for their work. If a disturbance or escape occurred the different accounts in these journals were worth comparing. If they had failed to fill in their books or their accounts were defective it could easily be spotted, for Sir George Paul saw to it that two 'visiting magistrates' were appointed to supervise each prison. They could enter it without warning at any time, check the journals, see the staff and inmates and then record their findings in their own journals.

Brief Summaries from Paul's Rule Book

The Chaplain. He is to take prayers Wednesdays and Fridays in the mornings and preach on Sundays. He is to keep a journal of his attendance and to visit any prisoner who asks to see him. He is to hold communion as often as he thinks fit. (This was rarely done as most prisoners felt too wicked to receive it.)

The Surgeon. He is to visit the sick daily and all the prisoners twice a week. He is to keep a journal on what he does for the sick.

Male felons. Get up at 6 a.m. in summer and at sunrise in winter; make beds; wash face and hands; go to chapel; roll call; prisoner's cleanliness to be checked and bread ration and 1d (to purchase what food they liked) to be given to those who are clean and were well-behaved in chapel. They are not allowed dogs, pigeons or poultry in the prison. Money games are forbidden. They must wear the prison uniform of yellow and blue.

Cells. To be equipped with iron bedsteads to allow for air circulation; straw mattresses; rug blanket; coarse linen sheets, which are to be changed weekly. Clean straw for mattresses weekly. Cells and galleries to be swept each morning and washed down once a week. Bedding to be put out for airing.

Q1 *Do magistrates act as 'visiting magistrates' in prisons today? What would they pay attention to on such a visit?*

Prisoners were dressed in yellow and blue uniforms, both to humiliate them and make them easy to spot if they escaped. Heads were shaved, but ankle irons soon proved to be unnecessary. They got 1.5 lb (0.67 kg) of bread daily and 1 pint (0.56 litres) of vegetable and meat soup twice a week . But they could buy more from a woman who went to the market for them. Hard labour was genuinely hard: it consisted of prison cleaning, making uniforms, sawing stone, polishing marble and other equally difficult tasks.

Sir George Paul's system won much praise from several teams of investigators over the years and formed the basis of other counties' reforms. The system was also copied in Cherry Hill Penitentiary, Philadelphia, and it was the American version which was to be 'imported' back to England by the government in a much stricter form as the Pentonville Model Prison in the nineteenth century (see p.144). Unfortunately the Pentonville system was a serious distortion of Sir George Paul's system. Many prisoners did leave Gloucester as reformed people, although some did return.

SPOTLIGHT   SPOTLIGHT

THE TREADWHEEL PROBLEM

When Sir George Paul died in 1820 the other magistrates felt that the prisoners ought to be dealt with more harshly. As a treadwheel had been introduced in other prisons they thought one was needed in Gloucester, the prison that the reformer had used as his model of what all prisons should be. Because it was used to grind corn or turn, it was designed so the wheel would not spin round too quickly

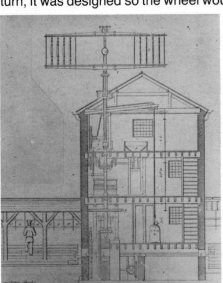

as the prisoner stepped onto it. The depth of the steps only allowed for a prisoner's toes. Men would do ten minutes on the wheel, followed by five minutes rest. The height of each step was 8 inches (203 mm) and one did 48 steps a minute which meant 18,000 steps a day over nine hours.The men hated it as it was such tiring work.

Part of the treadwheel at Gloucester Prison

CHAPTER 7

The Nineteenth Century

1. THE CRIMINAL CLASS

Contemporaries believed there was a definite Criminal Class which was not to be confused with the working class. Not all historians today agree there was such an obvious 'criminal class'. 'There is a distinct body of thieves . . . They may be known almost by their very gait in the streets,' wrote an unknown author in *Fraser's Magazine* in 1832. Of course there were people who committed a single crime in their lives (for example, the murder of a relative) who were not part of this class. By Criminal Class was meant those who lived by crime and who lived in certain areas of large cities. Entry to the Criminal Class gave the criminal the support of comrades, help in getting accommodation and access to receivers. Thus membership met a real need so far as criminals were concerned. 'I shall be all right when I find somebody to pal in with,' said an orphan released from gaol in 1876.

Bluegate Fields St., Georges'-in-the-East, London. Notice the single gaslight and the crowded street. Why are the people in this picture by the doorways?

> **Q1** *What ideas of right and wrong would criminals have which honest people could not accept?*

The Criminal Class tended to live in criminal areas of large cities known as rookeries. The worst rookery in London was St Giles' Parish with half a dozen streets, numerous alleyways and dark entries to small tenements, each with its way out in the back in case of emergency. Underground passages were said to link buildings. A third of London's beggars lived in St Giles'. Low public houses, lodging houses, coffee shops and cook-houses, known as 'flash-houses', were the places where gangs met. All served as centres for local information, for aiding released prisoners and for contacting receivers. The police knew these centres well, but they argued that if they were closed, then the police would not know where to find the criminals they were after!

Keepers of 'flash-houses' were often receivers, accepting a handkerchief for a dinner or a watch for a week's keep. Receivers would see to watches being 'christened', that is, given new maker's names, or having their mechanisms switched to avoid their being traced by their former owners.

THE DEALER IN OLD CLOTHES

TEACHING THE YOUNG IDEA HOW TO STEAL.

A cartoon from Punch, *1851. What does the sign on the door stand for? What do you think this man really does?*

Q1 *If you were a nineteenth-century chief constable, would you want 'flash-houses' closed or not? Why? Are there similar criminal centres today?*

Henry Mayhew wrote *London Labour and the London Poor* in four volumes (1851–62), about rookeries and all types of criminal. Here is an extract from his book:

> 'At the top of the Criminal Class were the 'Swell Mob'. Dressed well they would travel on cross-Channel ships in the spring to the continent before returning for the racing and fair season in Britain, ending the year at Manchester businessmen's gatherings. March-May were often spent in Wales at the fairs. They travelled in 1st class railway carriages to con the occupants. Thimble-riggers and card-sharps often wore clerical collars (see pp. 110–11). They took care of any of their fellows in prison by sending them presents and when they were released they would raffle something to raise money for them. A raffle of a silk handkerchief raised £2 13s 0d for Plummy Jukes which nearly covered the cost of his defence on a third pickpocketing charge.'

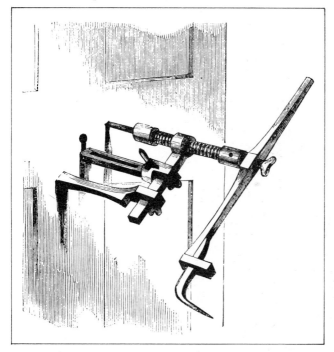

A jack-in-the-box, used by a nineteenth-century housebreaker to pull the lock out of a door

From what you have just read you can see that a number of people were convinced that a Criminal Class really did exist. But it is the historian's job to examine the records, such as those of courts, to check this claim. Thus Professor George Rudé found that although there was a minority of hardened criminals, a few gangs and some individual 'professionals', their number was not enough to use the phrase 'Criminal Class' to describe them.

Q1 *Write a newspaper article describing the haunts of the so-called Criminal Class and mention the types of thief you might meet.*

2. JUVENILE CRIME

The most striking thing about the Criminal Class in the first half of the nineteenth century was the large proportion that was under twenty years of age. Thomas Miller was first convicted at the age of eight in 1845, and by the age of twelve he had had eight convictions, five imprisonments and two whippings. A Liverpool delinquent was found to have had four aliases by the age of fourteen and been in custody 24 times, ranging from two to sixteen weeks at a stretch.

Orphans and abandoned children had really no alternative in life but to turn to crime. They slept under bridges, in house porches, in barrels or market pens. Twenty used to huddle up on the warm pavement outside the Whitechapel sugar bakery in the 1850s. Dr Barnardo reckoned there were 30,000 children sleeping rough in London in 1876. It was not only London criminals who began at a young age. Littledean Prison in the Forest of Dean had a regular supply of boys and girls of eight to fourteen years, some of whom found the care of Mrs Gunn, the keeper's wife, made prison more like home than anything they had known before.

Young children living rough in London, 1862

In court they liked to show off as 'bold and ardent sinners'. One observer remarked:

> 'I have seen young children, not in their 'teens', placed behind large iron bars, strong enough to restrain an elephant. And what is the effect? It is this: the mind of the boy becomes impressed with an idea that he must be a very clever lad to require such barricadoes [barricades], and that society has a great dread of his talents . . . The pomp and panoply [splendid show] of justice only gives these lads a feeling of self-importance: they never had any feeling of shame or disgrace.'

Dick Turpin and Jack Sheppard were these children's heroes. Adult thieves were only too happy to employ children to do the actual stealing under their direction.

John Binny described London child thieves like this:

> 'Some have no jacket, cap, or shoes, and wander about London with their ragged trousers hung by one brace; some have an old tattered coat, much too large for them, without shoes and stockings, and with one leg of the trousers rolled up to the knee; others have on an old greasy grey or black cap, with an old jacket rent at the elbows, and strips of the lining hanging down behind; others have on an old dirty pinafore; while some have petticoats. They aré generally in a squalid and unwashed condition, with their hair clustered in wild disorder like a mop, or hanging down in dishevelled locks, – in some cases cropped close to the head. . . . They are generally very acute and ready-witted, and have a knowing twinkle in their eye which exhibits the precocity of their minds. . . . A coat is suspended on the wall with a bell attached to it, and the boy attempts to take the handkerchief from the pocket without the bell ringing. Until he is able to do this with proficiency he is not considered well trained. Another way in which they are trained is this: The trainer – if a man – walks up and down the room with a handkerchief in the tail of his coat, and the ragged boys amuse themselves abstracting it until they learn to do it in an adroit manner.'

But there was to be a noticeable drop in juvenile crime from the 1850s onwards as leading gentry set up reformatory schools. In 1854 the Reformation Schools Act allowed courts to send young people under sentence of transportation or imprisonment to reformatories for two to five years. The government started to give grants to aid these schools. A Royal Commission in 1884 said they had 'broken up gangs of young criminals in larger towns; with putting an end to the training of boys as professional thieves; and with rescuing children fallen into crime from becoming habitual or hardened offenders'. Industrial schools could have children convicted of less serious offences sent to them from 1857 onwards.

Detaining them in a reformatory for two to five years as opposed to one to three months in prison meant a gang could lose its key member(s) for a long period. Hard labour ruined the finger delicacy they needed for picking pockets. Moreover employers were keen to take on ex-inmates as they had 'undergone a steady, regular training'. One point to notice is that boys in reformatory schools played cricket and football which poor children never did.

3. PATTERNS OF CRIME IN THE NINETEENTH CENTURY

There was probably an increase of crime in the first 30 years of the century, but the 'heroism' of violent crime then declined. Street robberies were bad in London until the Bow Street Runners reorganised their patrols in 1820. In the 1820s gas street-lighting was introduced in London, making mugging more difficult.

Highway robbery had largely gone from the London area by 1815. The start of the Bow Street Horse Patrol in 1805, the enclosure of Hounslow Heath, a general increase in traffic and more housing along London's approach roads made it too risky for the highwaymen. More turnpike gates meant more keepers who required bribes or were to be feared as informers. Contemporaries believed the increase in turnpikes was the main factor in ending highway robberies.

In 1830s crafty scheming came to replace violent daring in successful thieving. 'The modern thief depends upon his skill,' noted the *Cornhill Magazine* in 1862, while Charles Booth said both criminals and police saw violence as a breach of the 'rules of the game'. A short-lived exception was a wave of garrotting (theft by throttling) in 1862. A gang of three would grasp the victim. As two held the victim, the third would grab the man's neck, making him temporarily powerless to prevent the theft of his possessions. Flogging was hastily introduced as a penalty for this crime and it promptly died out. A marked drop in juvenile crime occurred from the 1850s with the start of the reformatories (see p. 109).

Thieving from ships anchored in the Thames was one of the main reasons for the building of the West and East India and London Docks from 1802–6. Cargo thefts dropped sharply, but Charles Dickens noted in 1853 that thieves called *lumpers* used large concealed pockets to steal small packages while *tier-rangers* listened for a captain's snores before robbing him.

But better communications also aided the thief as well as the police. Good roads meant a thief could leave London in the early evening in a hired light cart with fast horses, steal within a 12 to 30–kilometre radius and be home by early morning. He could hide the booty and get it collected by his innocent-looking girlfriend. Liverpool and Manchester thieves stole in each others' towns, as did thieves in Bristol and Bath.

Railways enabled thieves to get to race meetings or major social events easily. In the 1850s the London-Dover line was subject to crafty baggage thefts. The thief would stick a label for an intermediary station, say Croydon, over a label for Dover (or London) on a bag in the guard's van. He then got out at Croydon and claimed the bag, leaving the victim to discover his loss at the end of the journey!

The fact that there were no corridors to early carriages inevitably trapped a victim when he was set upon. When a Swiss tourist changed trains at

> **Q1** *List the factors reducing highway robbery in the order you think was most important. Why would the end of highway robbery mean the end of 'heroic' criminals?*

Bletchley, four well-dressed gentlemen showed him into a carriage and then tried to force him to play cards. When he declined they seized him by the throat and emptied his pockets. The Swiss escaped by pushing open the door and jumping out of the moving train. 'Can nothing be done to bring back the good old days of Dick Turpin, who was a brave and noble fellow compared with the cowardly brutes that infest our railways?', wrote a reader to the *Railway News*. Some worried railway companies decided to employ female detectives. A hushed London court heard one give evidence in 1885 against John Burgoyne charged with stealing a clergyman's bag. She said:

> 'By direction of the stationmaster I placed myself in the waiting-room and saw the prisoner come into the room. I saw him lift up a portmanteau [case] from beneath the table, put it down again, and go out on to the platform, but return almost immediately, and, taking up the portmanteau, go quickly out with it. He was dressed very shabbily, and had on shoes which prevented him being heard while walking. This excited my suspicions, and . . . I followed him.'

Burgoyne was found guilty. Novels chose trains as the scenes for assaults and murders and railway guidebooks warned passengers to watch out for suspicious characters.

A railway 'warning' notice of 1847

NEWCASTLE & CARLISLE RAILWAY.

CAUTION

TO THE PUBLIC.

A Person of the Name of HENRY O'NEIL was brought before JAMES KIRSOPP, Esquire, at the Magistrates' Office, Hexham, on Thursday the 18th Inst. charged with Travelling on the Newcastle and Carlisle Railway, between Wylam and Hexham, without having obtained a Ticket. The Charge was fully proved by the Company's Officers against the Prisoner, and the Magistrate convicted him in the Penalty of Twenty Shillings and Costs, besides the amount of the Fare for the entire Journey; and, in default of payment, he was committed to the House of Correction for Fourteen Days. Mr. Kirsopp, in the course of his address to the Prisoner, intimated his intention of increasing the severity of the Punishment in all future Cases which should be brought before him. He said the Company had placed Third Class Carriages upon their Line for the Benefit of the humbler Classes of Society, and these Cases of Fraud were certainly ungrateful acts.

The Directors are determined, by every means in their power, to detect any Party attempting to Defraud the Company, and have the Offenders visited with the severest Punishments authorized by their Act.—By Order,

JOHN ADAMSON,

Railway Office, Newcastle, 19th February, 1847.   CLERK TO THE COMPANY.

Newcastle-upon-Tyne: Printed at the Journal Office, 19, Grey-Street, by John Hernaman.

Q1 What effect do you think this notice had? What effect would similar publicity notices have today?

Q2 What different attitude to crime and punishment does this poster suggest compared to today's attitude? Keep in mind that in 1981, British Rail's Eastern Division lost £3 million (3 per cent of its total revenue) from fare dodging. Thirty-eight ticket inspectors detected 1,676 evasions; prosecutions numbered 970 and 92 per cent were successful, although the average fine was only £43.

Progress did not always favour the thief. The 1d post and the electric telegraph made it easier to catch criminals. Many thieves who thought they had out-distanced their pursuers found policemen waiting for them thanks to the telegraph system which allowed those left behind to wire ahead.

Counterfeiters in the 1820s faced difficulties as minting improved and became more difficult to copy. Metal buttons were no longer so fashionable, therefore depriving them of 'blanks' to use. However, when electroplating came in, in the 1850s, their equipment became lighter and therefore portable. Forging cheques, too, became more difficult when the banks started using different ink for the background. This meant that when the forger used eradicating fluid to remove the payee's name and the sum, leaving just the signature, he found the background was eradicated too!

The Fox Twins, Albert Ebenezer and Ebenezer Albert (b. 1857) were celebrated Hertfordshire poachers who between them collected 200 convictions for Game Law offences. They usually poached separately and escaped conviction many times when witnesses became confused over their identity. During their lives they had 50 weapons and miles of nets and wires confiscated. They lived in Woodbine Cottage, a home-made hut. They both courted the same girl, but she rejected them as she could not tell one from the other.

Photographing of prisoners started in Bristol in the 1850s and its value was soon appreciated. Fingerprinting came in in 1901 and as no two people in the world have similar prints this was a major step forward in crime detection. Look at the Fox Twins' prints.

4. CAUSES OF NINETEENTH-CENTURY CRIME

Poverty was not seen as the main cause of crime in the nineteenth century except in the years of adjustment after the battle of Waterloo, 1815, when the troops came home. In 1816 Robert Owen said, 'If the poor cannot procure employment, and are not supported, they must commit crimes or starve'. A Royal Commission in 1839 said crime was not caused by poverty, but by the attractions of a criminal life. Stealing had 'one common cause . . . the temptations of the profit'. In the mid-nineteenth century some people argued that the high cost of bread caused crime, but others disagreed. It was claimed that crime was higher in good times as more drink was consumed. Prison chaplain J.W. Horsley wrote in 1887, 'Our prison population rises with prosperity, and the consequent power of getting drink. Bad times and the slackness of work in winter produce less crime, not more.' Probably he was right, but it depends on which criminals are referred to. The so-called Criminal Class may have found more to steal in prosperous times. Previously honest people in hard times suffered a great deal before thieving at all; orphans and deserted or runaway children had to steal if starvation was the only alternative.

High birth and death rates in the nineteenth century meant that a lot of orphans and deserted children wandered the streets. Juvenile crime was closely linked to city rookeries. In 1828 101 out of 300 boys on the hulks were fatherless and 33 were motherless too. Sometimes parents simply lost control of their children who got into bad company while both parents worked hard to make ends meet. Lack of education was seen as a cause of crime. Others, however, said too much education would lead to frustration and crime if there were no jobs to be had. Revd. J.W. Horsley wrote, 'We find boys swindle and forge in a precocious manner, which is attributable not to ignorance but to instruction'. But school did keep children off the streets.

Drink played a big role in the life of the poor, both honest and criminal. It was seen as *a* – if not *the* – main cause of crime in the 1820s and 1830s. A drink, it was said, was needed before and after a crime. Certainly the proceeds of crime largely went on drink. Drink often brought newcomers into the Criminal Class as they committed assaults while drunk, or did a crime to buy drink.

Q1 *List the causes of nineteenth-century juvenile crime. List the causes of twentieth-century juvenile crime. What conclusions can you draw?*

Q2 *Is drink considered a cause of crime today? Look in the newspapers to see if anyone pleads he or she acted under the influence of drink. Do not forget to look at the road accident cases.*

The Black Maria, 1887. It was named after a strong Boston black woman who used to help police throw unruly customers out of her boarding house. It could hold ten people.

Drinking declined at the end of the nineteenth century as people were earning more steadily. Also temperance (anti-drink) movements such as the Evangelicals and the Salvation Army were making an impression on the public's outlook on the dangers of drink.

5. LAW AND ORDER

The Industrial Revolution's factories and new towns produced a law and order problem. The workers had to accept the long hours and low pay offered by their bosses. They even had to send their small children out to work to keep the family from starving. A class struggle between workers in and owners of industry was rapidly developing in the early nineteenth century. Only the JPs and parish constables stood ready to cope with any violence that would otherwise mean calling out the volunteer corps or the army. The violence began with Luddism and went on from 1811 to 1816.

Possibly named after Ned Ludlam, a Leicestershire apprentice who had once wrecked his machine when told off by a manager, the Luddite movement aimed to destroy new weaving machines. Craftsmen weavers felt these machines threatened both their status as skilled workers and eventually their jobs. They soon organised themselves into attack groups with hammer men to destroy the frames' ironwork, hatchet men to destroy the woodwork, musket men to stand guard and scouts to raise the alarm.

WHEREAS,

Several EVIL-MINDED PERSONS have assembled together in a riotous Manner, and DESTROYED a NUMBER of

FRAMES,

In different Parts of the Country :

THIS IS

TO GIVE NOTICE,

That any Person who will give Information of any Person or Persons thus wickedly

BREAKING THE FRAMES,

Shall, upon CONVICTION, receive

50 GUINEAS

REWARD.

And any Person who was actively engaged in RIOTING, who will impeach his Accomplices, shall, upon CONVICTION, receive the same Reward, and every Effort made to procure his Pardon.

☞ Information to be given to Messrs. COLDHAM and ENFIELD.

Nottingham, March 26, 1811.

G. Stretton, Printer, Nottingham.

Reward notice for frame breaking, 1811

Q1 *Name any groups of workers today who feel their livelihood or status is affected by new inventions. How are they drawing attention to the threat?*

It soon became clear that the middle-class constables, hastily enrolled by the JPs in Derbyshire, Nottinghamshire, Yorkshire and Lancashire, could not cope. They called on the volunteer corps. This only emphasised the class struggle, as the corps were really armed associations formed by wealthy employers. To show which side they were on, the government established a military camp for 3,000 regulars in the area to protect the plants from attack by dissatisfied workers.

Mr Cartwright knew his Rawfolds Mill in Yorkshire was threatened and he prepared it like a fortress. His 2.7 m-deep mill stream acted as a moat and the massive door was strengthened with heavy nails. He fixed 'rollers with spikes 16 to 18 inches [40.6 to 45.7 cm] in length' to the staircase and put large containers of vitriol at the top ready to pour down on any attackers. Very early on Sunday, 12 April 1812, 100 Luddites attacked Rawfords Mill, but Cartwright's four workmen and five soldiers had no difficulty in defending their fortress.

RAWFOLDS MILL.

Rawfolds Mill

Two Luddites were killed and the others fled. Their leader, George Mellor, was so desperate that he organised a small party to murder another mill owner, William Horsfall, as he rode home from Huddersfield. Mellor and two others were hanged in York as a result. Fourteen other Luddites were hanged for their rioting.

But the Luddites had forced the government to use 12,000 troops and hundreds of spies and informers to restore order. The troops had been posted in town pubs, selected villages and at obvious targets for attack. Cavalry troops of 40 to 100 strong had patrolled extensively. Spies, some locally recruited, infiltrated the Luddites so that they dared not trust each other. These spies became an essential aid to keeping law and order in the absence of a police force. In spite of all the disruption, the connection between distress and disorder was hardly recognised.

Thus local disorders immediately became emergencies, needing desperate emergency measures to cope with them. The generals in charge of the troops repeatedly said that a permanent police force would have been much more effective than their troops. At first MPs favoured such a force, but they soon lost interest as the trouble died down. They dismissed the Luddites as a group of backward-looking troublemakers and failed to see them as the forerunners of working-class revolutionaries. In fact the Luddites were moderate, loyal men who had found violence was the only way to express their despair, for they had no vote and consequently no MPs to support working-class aims.

How could violence be stopped? If the workers' pay and hours were improved they would not rebel. But in those days governments did not make laws on minimum wages or conditions of work. The only alternative the government had was swift punishment for the ringleaders. This depended on spies finding out who they were. Spy Oliver, an ex-debtor, became the government's best *agent provocateur* (someone who provokes others to take action in order to trap or inform on them) in 1817. He was behind the 'March of the Blanketeers', and the Pentrich Uprising in 1817. In both he talked simple-minded workers into believing revolution was possible. Encouraged by him, they walked into the traps set for them by the JPs and the troops. Although MPs called for an end to such provocation, the government relied on its spies too much to give in to their demands. A parliamentary committee warned MPs in 1818 that a continental-type police force would mean more spying. It would be 'odious and repulsive . . . [and] make every servant of every house a spy on the actions of his master, and all classes of society spies on each other'. Again the real solution of democratic representation through the ballot box was brushed aside.

6. THE PETERLOO MASSACRE, 1819

St Peter's Field, Manchester, was the setting for a meeting of 60,000 to demand that the 'village' of Manchester receive a town's charter and the right to elect MPs. The JPs could not believe such a gathering would be peaceful and so had enrolled 400 constables and stationed 1,500 troops and volunteer corps' yeomanry nearby. When the meeting opened, the authorities read the Riot Act and called in the Manchester Yeomanry Cavalry. This middle-class band had been drinking while they waited to

> **Q1** *Imagine that you are a Yorkshire MP of that period. Explain to Parliament the connection between distress and disorder. Say what you think should be done.*

be summoned. Now they charged through the crowd, knocking a baby from its mother's arms. Confusion followed when the Yeomanry, untrained in crowd control, used the cutting edges of their sabres. One man's life was saved from a blow by the cheese he had put inside his hat, but another had his nose cut off. Seeing the chaos, the JPs sent in the regular troops, who used the flat sides of their sabres to beat back the crowd and rescue the Yeomanry. It seems possible that fifteen people were killed and 421 injured, including 100 women; 67 troops were slightly hurt. Some of the crowd, who had fought at Waterloo in 1815, christened the massacre 'Peterloo'. The government had to support the action of the JPs. Six 'Gagging Acts' were passed in 1819. These acts prevented seditious meetings of more than 50; allowed JPs to search houses for weapons and seize seditious pamphlets; and made the drilling of demonstrators illegal.

MANCHESTER HEROES

The Manchester Yeomanry Cavalry act like butchers. Their officer encourages them to reduce the poor rates by killing the poor.

But the massacre made some middle- and upper-class people realise that some modest parliamentary reform was now essential to give the workers a means of expressing their grievances peacefully.

Q1 *Write a playlet in which a member of the Manchester Yeomanry Cavalry meets a member of the crowd in a pub a week after the Massacre.*

Q2 *Do you think governments should use spies in Britain? If so, under what circumstances and what instructions would you give them?*

CATO STREET CONSPIRACY, 1820

The government's use of *agents provocateurs* was to reach its highest point when George Edwards was made second-in-command in Arthur Thistlewood's revolutionary band for their *West End Job*. Edwards had had an unusual upbringing. His first job consisted of selling models of Eton College's headmaster to pupils for target practice! He sent his reports to the Home Office on strips of paper 5 cm wide and about 45 cm long. He reported the group's code words: guns = speaks; pistols = tellers; swords = thrusts; pikes = mows.

The aim of Thistlewood's band was to murder the cabinet and form a revolutionary government. Edwards suggested to the group the blowing up of the Commons, but Thistlewood did not want to kill innocent people. Murder them at a fête, suggested Edwards, but Thistlewood protested that there would be ladies present! Finally they decided to murder the cabinet members while they were dining at Lord Harrowby's house. Pikes were made of broomsticks and old bayonets and home-made 'fire balls' prepared. One conspirator brought a sack to put the ministers' heads in. Just as the band was preparing to leave their upstairs hideout in Cato Street, the Bow Street Runners burst in. A desperate fight followed and one Runner was killed. The band were soon rounded up and eleven, including a butcher, a baker, a carpenter and six cobblers, were charged with treason. Their defence counsel argued that the whole plot was too absurd to be real! In the end five were sentenced to hanging, drawing and quartering, but this was changed to decapitation after hanging.

A vast crowd watched the executions and troops were everywhere. A masked man cut off the heads after the men had hung for some while. When the heads were held up high, one bled a lot and another was dropped. The crowd were livid. The bodies were buried in the underground tunnel linking Newgate with the Old Bailey. The lesser members of the gang were transported to Australia and one, a shoemaker, eventually became chief constable of Bathurst.

Questions were asked in Parliament about the whereabouts of Edwards and his role in the affair. He had been smuggled to Guernsey and on to Cape Town where he changed his name. In his absence a grand jury found a treason bill against him. The point is that without his encouragement the plot would never have been made. This raised the question of who was the real criminal, Edwards or Thistlewood? The government was content to give generous rewards to the Bow Street Runners, but they knew that it would be unwise to use *agents provocateurs* again.

The Cato Street conspirators fight the Bow Street Runners (see the Spotlight on the previous page)

7.   THE GREAT REFORM BILL RIOTS, 1831

The Great Reform Bill was intended to do away with much of the corruption at elections and bring about parliamentary reforms. When it ran into difficulties in Parliament, there was an outburst of rioting. At Bristol the JPs dared not order the troops to fire, while the troops did not dare to do so without the JPs' orders. The result was three days of rioting. Afterwards ten JPs were charged with neglecting their duty in failing to order the troops to fire or mustering a sufficient force to tackle the rioters. Their defence was that they had tried to call out the *posse comitatus* by putting notices on church doors and appealing for volunteers. Only 150 out of 100,000 recognised their duty under the Statute of Winchester, 1285. The JPs were acquitted. The judge pointed out that JPs were trapped between a possible murder charge if they exceeded their duties and one of neglect if they did not perform their duties. Col. Brereton, in charge of the troops, committed suicide before his trial. He had panicked and bargained with the rioters to withdraw his troops if they dispersed. The delighted rioters had simply continued the destruction when the troops withdrew!

> **Q1** *Which eighteenth-century riots would the Bristol JPs and the colonel have remembered and why?*
>
> **Q2** *What were the main points of the Statute of Winchester? What was meant by 'posse comitatus'?*

8. SIR ROBERT PEEL AND THE METROPOLITAN POLICE ACT, 1829

Sir Robert Peel, founder of the Metropolitan Police

Home Secretary Sir Robert Peel (1788–1850) was responsible for re-modelling London's police force. When he took office there was a variety of constables, one constable for every 3,000 people. Today there is one for every 300.

It took time to persuade Parliament to pass the Metropolitan Police Act and Peel had to omit the City of London in the centre of the capital from the scope of the act. It gave him control of policing within a rough circle seven miles from the centre. This was extended to fifteen miles in 1839. Some 3,000 men were to be recruited by two Commissioners of Police. The Commissioners were Col. Sir Charles Rowan, who was used to commanding men, and Richard Mayne, a lawyer, who was good at drawing up regulations. Working from a house backing on to Scotland Yard, they divided London up into seventeen divisions, each with a company of 144 constables under a superintendent. Policemen had to be under 35 years of age, at least 5ft 7in (1.7 m) tall, healthy and able to read and write. Most of those who joined were ex-soldiers. Many expected to be allowed to use umbrellas in rainy weather!

Of the first 2,800, 2,200 were eventually dismissed or resigned. Pay was low. Those who joined tended to be working-class people rather than the middle class who had previously joined the volunteer corps. Their uniform was designed to make them look like civilians. They were to operate on the beat system, that is, patrolling a set area. This meant walking twenty miles a day, seven days a week. They had no special protection from the law for any action they took. In other words if they overreacted they could be in serious trouble. They were taught that success depended on the public approving of them. Otherwise, they would be at the mercy of the mob. Prestige and persuasion, not power, were the keys to success.

*Sir Charles Rowan (1783–1852),
Commissioner 1829–50*

*Sir Richard Mayne (1796–1868),
Commissioner 1829–68*

Metropolitan Police: inspector on the left; policeman on the right. They wore dark blue uniforms with white or light grey trousers in summer. The trousers cost 2s. (10p). Their hats were made of rabbit-skin and covered with leather. Their cane frames were a protection from attack and made it possible for them to be used for standing on in order to look over walls, etc. They weighed 510 g and were unhealthy as they had no vents. The men carried truncheons and rattles. Whistles were issued in 1884. The striped armlet was worn when on duty.

Q1 *Why do you think members of the Metropolitan Police were called 'Bobbies' or 'Peelers'?*

The 'Peelers' were not readily accepted by the public. When they tried to control traffic, coach owners tried to run them down. Newspapers complained of brutal assaults on innocent citizens when they made arrests, and neglect of duty when they failed to do so. JPs resented their own lack of control over the new force and obstructed them in court. The worst case came in 1833 when PC Robert Culley was stabbed to death helping to quell a riot by the National Political Union of the Working Classes. The inquest verdict given was 'justifiable homicide' and the jury got a dinner and a medal each. Parliament made an investigation and found the police blameless. A public subscription was raised for Culley's widow.

Peel's Police,
RAW LOBSTERS,
Blue Devils,

Or by whatever other appropriate Name they may be known.

Notice is hereby given,

That a Subscription has been entered into, to supply the **PEOPLE** with **STAVES** of a superior Effect, either for Defence or Punishment, which will be in readiness to be gratuitously distributed whenever a similar unprovoked, and therefore unmanly and bloodthirsty Attack, be again made upon Englishmen, by a Force unknown to the British Constitution, and called into existence by a Parliament illegally constituted, legislating for their individual interests, consequently in opposition to the Public good.

Anti-police propaganda, 1830

Q1 *When had a jury who had given a verdict against established authority been treated in the same way in the eighteenth century?*

Q2 *Explain in your own words what 'justifiable homicide' means.*

Strangely it was one of the radical leaders of the day, Francis Place, who solved the problem of riot control. Anxious that his meetings should not be disrupted by mobs, he suggested the baton charge. It was an immediate success.

The Metropolitan Police Act of 1839 ended the Bow Street Runners, their Horse Patrol and the Thames Police as separate forces under JPs. The act also extended the Metropolitan Police's control to a fifteen-mile (24 km) radius from Charing Cross.

9. POLICING OUTSIDE LONDON

But what of policing new cities like Liverpool in 1834 with 250,000 people and 50 nightwatchmen? Many places had formed property owners' organisations to fight crime. Gloucestershire had fifteen such associations which used their subscription money to prosecute criminals.

'Peelers' were loaned by the Metropolitan Police to local associations outside London who were prepared to pay for them. This was considered cheaper than starting town or county police forces by paying for them out of the rates. But the Municipal Corporations Act of 1835 required towns to set up forces in the way they thought best. When half had done nothing three years later the government passed the County Police Act of 1839. County forces were to be under the control of Quarter Sessions which would decide the size of the force, and appoint and dismiss its chief constable. Despite this new act, only 24 counties complied and set up police forces. The government responded to this refusal to act on the counties' part in 1856 with the County and Borough Police Act. It insisted forces be set up. One policeman per 1,000 of population in a county was the rule. Government grants were to be given for forces reported efficient by inspectors of constabulary.

The act was denounced as a threat to liberty and fears were expressed that the Home Secretary would use government spies to combat free political expression. In fact the existence of 239 separate forces all with varying recruiting procedures, pay, pensions, uniforms and working hours prevented the government using them for political purposes which might have threatened people's liberty. The only things the forces had in common were the beat system, an annual inspection and a Home Office grant. County rates were doubled by the cost of these forces. The creation of new county councils in 1888 led to county forces being supervised by Standing Joint Committees, that is to say, committees made up of JPs and councillors.

Q1 *Can you explain what a 'baton charge' is and why it should be successful?*

CHARTISTS' NEWPORT UPRISING, NOVEMBER, 1839

The Chartist movement aimed at parliamentary reform. They advocated that working men should vote and become MPs. Most members of the organisation tried to achieve these aims by presenting huge petitions to Parliament, but others decided to use force. This led to the passing of the County Police Act, 1839, allowing counties to start police forces.

The Westgate Hotel in Newport, Monmouthshire, was the scene of the biggest class-war battles of the century. The miners and ironworkers of the valleys were led by John Frost, Zephaniah Williams and William Jones on a damp midnight march to rescue an imprisoned Chartist leader and start the insurrection which they hoped would sweep through Britain. Frost called on them to have 'recourse to the ancient institutions of our country' by forming tithings, as Chartists in Scotland and the Midlands were doing. But they spent too long marshalling their men and arrived in daylight. The mayor read the Riot Act and then the troops he had stationed in the hotel flung the shutters open and fired into the crowd. Twenty-two were killed and many wounded. The three ringleaders were charged with high treason and would have been executed had the trial judge not told the Home Secretary that they had not really committed that particular offence for which they were tried. They were transported for life, although pardoned in 1855. Frost alone returned home to a hero's welcome.

The attack by Chartists on the Westgate Hotel, Newport

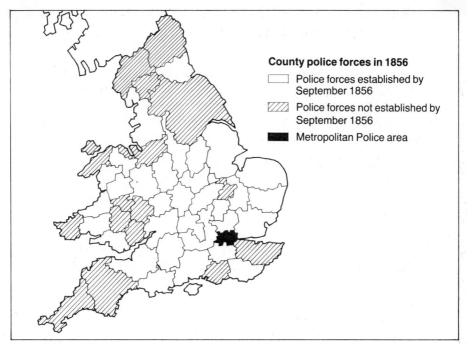

County police forces in 1856

☐ Police forces established by September 1856

▨ Police forces not established by September 1856

■ Metropolitan Police area

Metropolitan PC Andrews' weekly budget, 1853

	£	s	d		£	s	d
Wages	1	1	0	Sugar			8
Rent		4	6	Other food, but not meat		3	11
Bread		5	0	Wood, candles, coal		1	8
Flour		1	0	School fees			4
Tea		1	0				

That left him with 3s 4d to pay for clothing, medicine, etc. for himself, his wife and five children.

By the 1870s agricultural workers made up 33 per cent of the Metropolitan Police's recruits and 13 per cent of the armed forces. Free houses for members of the Metropolitan Police were available from the 1890s. Outside London, pay varied widely from one force to another, but members had little chance of contacting each other and discovering this. Leave varied from one unpaid week to two paid weeks a year. Policemen were not allowed to leave their homes in off-duty hours without permission, but they were allowed to do off-duty work such as doormen at weddings to increase their pay. They worked a seven-day week until 1908. Tiredness and the unhealthy areas in which police stations were built led to much sickness amongst the members of many forces. Nevertheless, the policemen were often expected to double-up as the local fire service. In one town the station's corridor had two lines of pegs, one lot for police coats and hats and the other for the fire service ones! Promotion exams came in in the 1860s.

REBECCA RIOTS, 1839–43

...th West Wales was the centre of the anti-turnpike riots. Five ...rnpikes led to Carmarthen and when the Whitland Trust put up a new tollgate at Efailwen in time to collect tolls from the lime carts heading for the kilns at Ludchurch, it set off strong resistance. The gate was attacked three times from May to July, 1839. Each time it was destroyed. On the second occasion, 400 men with blackened faces and many dressed in female clothing assaulted it. On the third occasion the leader was the prize-fighting local farmer Thomas Rees, better known as Twm Carnabwth. It is said he borrowed the clothes of a stout woman called Rebecca. Further trouble occurred in 1842 and spread to neighbouring areas. In 1843 a crowd ransacked the Carmarthen workhouse. Troops and special constables were moved into the area. The leaders both received heavy sentences: John Jones (Shoni Sgubor Fawr) got transportation for life and David Davies (Dai'r Cantwr) for twenty years. A report by a Royal Commission on Welsh turnpikes in 1844 led to the standardisation of tolls and a reduction in lime-cart tolls.

An artist's impression of the Rebecca rioters in The Illustrated London News

A map of the Rebecca Riots

10. EARLY DETECTIVES

Detective work was not the strong point of the early forces. Plain-clothes policemen reminded people of government spies. In 1833, Sgt Popay disguised himself as a worker and joined the National Political Union of the Working Classes to see if it were plotting a revolution. When union members spotted him in a police station there was a great outcry and he was dismissed as an *agent provocateur*. After the Bow Street Runners were disbanded in 1839, there was no detective force until 1842 when eight detectives were appointed. In 1867 the members of a secret Irish American revolutionary society called the Fenians, which was intent on throwing the British out of Ireland, tried to rescue two of their supporters from Clerkenwell Prison. The attempt made the public see the need for detectives able to gather intelligence on such groups.

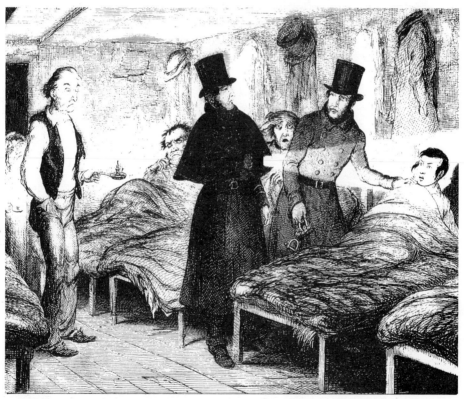

A robber is arrested in a cheap lodging house. From George Cruikshank's The Drunkard's Children, *1848*

In 1877 the CID (Criminal Investigation Department) was increased to 200 men and in 1883 to 800. Irish dynamiting of the Tower, Parliament and underground stations led to the formation of the Special Irish Branch in 1884. Two detectives infiltrated the gang just before it could strike at Queen Victoria's Golden Jubilee in 1887.

A Victorian detective, Superintendent Adolphus Williamson. In 1877 he found that a gang of swindlers who deprived a woman of £30,000 had bribed two of his inspectors. The inspectors were later sent to prison.

Jack the Ripper. This murderer wrote letters to the police about a series of knife murders he had committed in the East End of London in 1888, signing them 'Jack the Ripper'. His victims had their throats cut and their bodies mutilated. He was never caught.

Q1   *How could one justify using Special Branch men to protect the Queen's Golden Jubilee? How did the detectives differ from* agents provocateurs? *Is telephone tapping today ever justified?*

11. METROPOLITAN POLICE VERSUS DEMONSTRATORS

Were the new police set up at this time able to control large bodies of demonstrators? A description of three violent incidents provides conflicting answers.

CHARTISTS PRESENT THEIR THIRD PETITION FOR PARLIAMENTARY REFORM, 10 APRIL 1848

The Chartists planned to gather on Kennington Common (now the Oval) which could hold 54,000, and march across Westminster Bridge to the Houses of Parliament. The Duke of Wellington took charge of defending the capital, making use of the new telegraph system to follow the Chartists' movements. The Duke did not consider the 1,000 police and 180,000 'specials' adequate for the task. He enlisted 7,000 troops and 1,300 Chelsea Pensioners (former soldiers living on a government pension), and had field guns put on river steamers to bombard the Chartists as they crossed the bridge. The knowledge of Wellington's preparations unnerved Feargus O'Connor, the Chartists' leader. He called off the march as the rain poured down.

THE REFORM LEAGUE'S 'MONSTER' HYDE PARK MEETING, 23 JULY 1866

This meeting was to claim that 'intelligent and honest men' had a right to assemble anywhere. Over 1,600 policemen guarded the locked park gates. Some demonstrators turned back, but others tore down the railings. Many policemen were seriously hurt and the troops had to be called out. In 1872 Parliament recognised the right of demonstrators to meet in Hyde Park. Soap-box orators use it to this day.

Hyde Park, 23 July 1866, from The Illustrated London News

'BLOODY SUNDAY', TRAFALGAR SQUARE, 13 NOVEMBER 1887

The Social Democratic Federation sought to secure the right to demonstrate peacefully in Trafalgar Square. Unemployed people had been gathering round the Red Flag each day for more than a month, with 2,000 policemen supervising the crowd each day. Reluctantly the Home Secretary had agreed to the Commissioner's request to close the Square. His request was strongly denounced in the press as 'an outrage on . . . rights and liberties'.

'Specials' being instructed for use on 'Bloody Sunday' 1887

Truncheon inscribed 'Trafalgar Square Riot, 1887, J.S.Whiting, Special Constable'

The *Pall Mall Gazette* called the Commission 'a soldier in jackboots' surrounding the Square with his 'police cavalry' and having 'troops with ball cartridge ready to massacre an unarmed populace'. Large numbers of young city workers were made special constables and given truncheons. In the end they and the police managed to contain the riot, although two squadrons of Life Guards and 400 footguards were brought up in readiness. Seventy-seven policemen were injured and two of the crowd died. *The Reynolds News* claimed that:

> 'The brutal police proceedings of last Sunday . . . will never fade . . . from the memory of any actual beholder . . . Peaceable citizens . . . were . . . ruthlessly ridden down by mounted blackguards and bludgeoned by police infantry, as if they had been a gang of mutineers or daring burglars'.

As a precaution, the Home Secretary told JPs to swear in 20,000 special constables for two months. The crowd returned the following Sunday, but the meeting passed off quietly. Today the Home Secretary's permission is needed to hold meetings in the Square.

'Bloody Sunday', Trafalgar Square

Constables on the beat did cut down street crimes such as picking pockets and mugging. Requests for patrols from tradesmen, farmers and suburban householders showed their presence was valued. In fact the

Q1 *Did the Metropolitan Police prove adequate to control the Chartists' march planned for 10 April 1848?*

Q2 *How did the authority's plans for dealing with the Hyde Park Meeting differ from those for dealing with the Chartists' demonstration of 10 April 1848?*

Q3 *Find out if any political meetings have been held in Trafalgar Square recently. How was order maintained at them?*

Q4 *If you were the Home Secretary, what factors for and against allowing a political demonstration to take place would you need to consider?*

propertied classes generally welcomed them. The working class varied in its feelings towards them, and still does as the 1984 miners' strike showed clearly.

The all-important question was who was going to control and finance the police? In 1844 the Manchester police cost the ratepayers £23,000, which was three times the value of property stolen that year. The start of county forces often doubled the rates. But from 1856 the government paid 25 per cent of the costs and from 1874, 50 per cent. Control, however, was left in local hands – borough Watch Committees and county Standing Joint Committees – who employed their forces. A central police force used by the government or property owners to maintain political or economic control did not therefore emerge in Britain, as many had feared. If it had, our liberties would be much less than they are today.

12. BRINGING A PROSECUTION IN THE EARLY NINETEENTH CENTURY

At the beginning of the nineteenth century prosecutions still had to be arranged, and often conducted, by the victim. Only slowly, as police forces became established, did the police begin to bring prosecutions on behalf of the victim. The appointment of a Director of Public Prosecutions did not occur until 1879 (see p. 141). So what would encourage or discourage a victim from bringing a prosecution – assuming he or she had someone to accuse? Until 1818 there was the temptation of Parliamentary Rewards of £40 to cover the costs of a successful prosecution. But it was a much-disliked system. Parliamentary Rewards deterred people from prosecuting unless they could be sure of getting the £40. An 1818 act allowed the court to pay expenses and additional rewards in felony cases when it felt it was justified.

But the difficulties with bringing a prosecution could be daunting. No dates for trials were fixed, so that you and your witnesses had to wait for up to two weeks when the Assizes or Quarter Sessions began. This meant you and they would lose earnings for the period. The accused or his associates might seek revenge too. The accused also often got off on a technical point. For example, a man escaped conviction in 1845 when it was spotted that the name of a JP who had formerly convicted him was spelt 'Dalivon' on one document and 'Dalison' on another. No wonder law-abiding people formed local Associations for the Prosecutions of Offenders (see p. 125). Gradually courts were allowed to amend such documentary errors provided they were only slip-ups.

Q1 *Explain why the public was reluctant to have the new police. Why did it come to accept them in the end?*

LIFE, TRIAL, AND EXECUTION
OF JAMES GREENACRE,

With a Copy of a Letter addressed to Mrs. Greenacre in America.

INTERIOR OF THE

CHAPEL OF NEWGATE.

This man after a lengthened Trial, which lasted two days, viz. the 10th and 11 days of April, the particulars of which we gave in former publications, was found guilty of the Wilful Murder of Hannah Brown, to whom, as was supposed, he was to have been married

The only confession he made as can possibly be relied on, was as follows, though he had private communications with Mr. Cotton, and Mr. M'Murdo, the Chaplin and Surgeon of Newgate

When the Recorder had passed sentence upon Greenacre, he appeared to be very uneasy, and asked to see one of the turnkeys, he was accordingly waited on, when he stated, that when himself and Mrs. Brown entered his apartments in Carpenters Buildings, they had words concering the deception that had been resorted to, by both parties, when she being very agrievating, he took up a piece of wood, resembling a jack-towel-roller, and gave her a blow over the eye ; she was then in the act of falling, but caught her and placed her in a chair, then took a knife and run it across her throat, and placed a peil by her side to catch the blood. He then sat down to consider in what way he should dispose of the body ; many plans occured to him, but he decided on cutting it up, and disposing of it any way possible. He severed the head and legs from the trunk, and carried the head to Mrs Davis's in Bartholomew-close, (who in her evidence it will be remembered stated that Greenacre had a bag with what she supposed to be a quartern loaf in it), where he stoped until about 11 o'clock on the same evening as the deed was committed, (Christmas-eve), and then hastened on to

Stepney, and threw it in the Regent's-canal, near the locks. He could then proceed no futher, but protested to the innocence of Gale.

LETTER.

Chapel Yard, Newgate,
April 30, 1837.

Dear Louisa,

I am sorry you should have to upbraid me with having forgotten the duties of a husband, but assure you from the hour I took my farewell of you, (which was then my intention to have b en but for a short period), through the treachery of those who termed themselves friends, I have been involved in difficulties, which has at length proved a fatal result, some idea of which you may form by noticing from whence this is directed.

There is no occasion, dear girl, for me to enter into the particulars concerning the cause of my lamentable end, as you will, if you have not already, through the medium of the press, which has in every particular, endeavoured to blacken my character, undeservedly. However, I freely forgive all, as I hope to be forgiven, not only by man, but by my Almighty God, to whom, I hope, you will fervently pray on my behalf.

Receive, dear girl, the blessing of your ilfated and forlorn Husband,
JAMES GREENACRE.
P.S. Long ere this reaches you, I shall be no more.

EXECUTION.

This morning, at a very early hour, the houses facing, and all the avenues leading to the goal, were crowded with persons anxiously awaiting the fatal time which would assuredly terminate this wretched man's wicked career. At a quarter to 8 o'clock, the hangman appeared on the gallows, and prepared the rope, noose, &c. and at 8 o'clock, the Prisoner, attended by the Sheriff, and Chaplin, came forward in solemn procession, and was then shortly launched into eternity.

COPY OF VERSES.

All you who walk in follies path,
　Attention give to me,
And listen to the tale I tell
　Of my sad destiny !
In that genial pleasant month,
　When nature looks so gay,
I'm doom'd to die a wretched death
　On the second day of May.

Hard is my fate, for all will point
　With contempt and scorn,
Not one will heave a sigh for me
　Upon the fatal morn.
Must I die as a murderer,
　O, shocking is the thought,
To own a crime so very black,
　I never can be brought.

Thus spoke this wretched man, my friends,
　When he his sentence heard ;
He fears not God, he loves not truth,
　In all he acts absurd.
Then let us pray to God that we
　All deeds like this may shun,
And keep within a virtuous path
　'Til our race is run.

May all who ever acted wrong,
　Hence change their wretched plan,
Greenacre's case a warning prove
　To woman, child, and man.
All praise your God, and raise your voice,
　To shout his holy name,
Trust but in him, you need not fear
　You'll end your days in shame.

Printed and Published by J. V QUICK, Bowling Green Lane, Clerkenwell.

Broadsheet of the life, trial and execution of James Greenacre (1837)

Still other difficulties remained. A thief might use a go-between (often a policeman!) to return stolen goods at a price. And even if you got your case sufficiently prepared, the grand jury had to find a 'True Bill' against the accused before the trial could start. These juries met in secret. You could not present (explain) the case to them. They simply heard what prosecution witnesses had to say and sorted the case out for themselves. The accused might get a false witness to offer evidence which conflicted with that of the others. It was little wonder that London thieves were great supporters of the grand jury system! It was not abolished until 1933.

However, as the century progressed the police not only helped more with prosecutions, but they also provided protection from reprisals. Also a number of government acts transferred the hearing of some crimes to summary jurisdiction, that is, trial by JP without juries being involved. This meant justice could be obtained more cheaply and swiftly.

The marked reduction in the number of crimes liable to the death sentence greatly encouraged courts to find the accused guilty. Previously, many juries had been reluctant to convict even when they knew the accused was guilty because they felt the punishment of death was too great for a minor felony. Prosecutors, knowing juries' reluctance to convict, were reluctant to prosecute. From 1805 to 1814, none of the 80 convicted at the Old Bailey for shoplifting were executed. From 1828 to 1834, of 8,483 persons sentenced to death in England and Wales, only 355 (or less than 5 per cent) were executed. As death penalties were withdrawn from one crime after another during the century, there was no increase in crime. In fact there were more convictions in relation to the number of committals. By the mid-nineteenth century people were arguing about whether capital punishment should be maintained for murder if it was unpremeditated.

13. JPs IN THE NINETEENTH CENTURY

The problem of the trading JPs of the eighteenth century (see p. 65) had led in 1792 to the start of a system of paid magistrates who were lawyers to handle cases in London. They were called police magistrates and later, stipendiaries (stipend = a salary). Some people saw them as paid government agents as they sat alone and had the authority of two JPs sitting together; they still do today. From 1839 they had to be barristers of seven years' standing before they could be appointed. One MP said this would be a 'blow to the existence of the unpaid magistracy, who have long been the boast of England'. Today a number of large cities, besides London, have stipendiaries.

> **Q1** *In 1986, a court refused to extradite a woman wanted on a bombing charge because the papers requesting her extradition were incorrectly drawn up. Do you think courts should let someone off because of a technicality?*

Another change made to ensure that JPs provided good justice came in 1848–9 when they were required to hold their Petty Sessions in 'an open and public place to which the public generally may have access'.

As the nineteenth century began, more members of the aristocracy became involved in Quarter Sessions work. Possibly a quarter of the JPs in counties were Church of England clergymen who now considered both the job of JP and prison reform as part of their pastoral work. In some counties the majority of JPs were clergy.

Benches were particularly concerned to see that property was protected. As the sport of shooting came to be taken more seriously, new Game Laws stiffened penalties for poaching. In spite of the fact that poaching usually increased when the price of bread was high, the penalty of transportation was given for those caught at night. County JPs did not face up to the connection between poverty and crime. They were criticised for their tough use of the Game Laws. H. Brougham said in 1828, 'There is not a worse . . . tribunal on the face of the earth than that . . . at which . . . convictions on the Game Laws take place . . . I mean . . . a brace of sporting magistrates'.

A poacher up before the beak (JP). His wife and child plead for mercy.

Gloucestershire's South Cerney and Littledean were poaching communities where almost everyone was involved in crime. In 1844 thirty gamekeepers were killed throughout the county.

Q1 *What kind of abuses by JPs did open sessions prevent?*

Q2 *Find out if any clergy are JPs in your area today.*

Q3 *Answer the following questions: (a) Would the poacher have got a fairer hearing in an open court? (b) What is on the table? (c) What does that tell us about the atmosphere in the room? (d) What is the job of the man holding the rabbit?*

Twice a year the county's JPs gathered to greet the assize judges when they came round on circuit to hear serious cases. This enabled the judges to give them any advice or instructions from London. This might involve a campaign against a particular crime. The judges could check on business done at the last Quarter Sessions or see how the prison was managed. JPs also reported their problems or experiments to the judges. In short, a partnership based on the better providing of justice was established.

14. REFORMING THE LAW

JEREMY BENTHAM (1748–1832)

Bentham was a famous philosopher who had trained as a lawyer. He called for the modernising of the whole legal system. He said it was too expensive for people to turn to; there were not enough local courts within reach; and the jargon used was too technical for people to understand, as it was often in Latin or French. Grand juries, in his opinion, were no longer needed and the system of charging fees for writs and hearing cases and so on should end. Behind all his comments lies the question he always asked himself, 'What use is it?'. He meant useful in promoting the greatest happiness of the greatest number of people. The aim of having the law and the courts, he argued, was to help people get justice, not hinder them from doing so.

Bentham's main achievement was to draw up a set of principles on which to base a reform of the legal system. He divided criminal offences into four classes according to the amount of injury a criminal caused to (a) individuals, (b) himself, (c) classes or groups, and (d) the general public.

He listed thirteen rules for penalties. For example, the harm caused by a punishment must not be greater than that caused by the offence. But the suffering caused by the punishment must be slightly greater than the benefit the criminal expected to get from the crime.

Three men were deeply influenced by Bentham's teachings: Sir Robert Peel, Sir Samuel Romilly and Lord Brougham.

Q1 *Find out how the partnership between JPs and judges works today.*

Q2 *What hindrances to justice did Bentham pinpoint?*

Q3 *List different crimes to fit these classes. What do you think of dividing criminal offences into such classes?*

Q4 *Following Bentham's guidelines for penalties, what punishments would be suitable for (a) theft of washing from a line, and (b) murder? What punishments were then given for these offences?*

Q5 *Bentham said the Anglo-Saxon wergild was unfair as the punishment might not compare with the gain the criminal made. Reread the discussion about wergild and try to explain what he meant.*

SIR ROBERT PEEL (1788–1850)

During his period as Home Secretary starting in 1822, Peel reduced 300 criminal laws to four comprehensive ones. He abolished jail fees, standardised the classification of prisoners, appointed women warders to female prisons, and abolished the benefit of clergy and branding. He also allowed pleas of 'not guilty' to be recorded on those who refused to plead and allowed judges to give less than the death sentence for non-killing capital offences. He reduced eight acts on recruiting juries to one act and 92 acts on theft (which accounted for sixth-sevenths of crime) to one of 30 pages. He stopped the death penalty for over 100 offences.

SIR SAMUEL ROMILLY (1757–1818)

Romilly, whose nanny had read him the *Newgate Calendar* at bedtime, became Solicitor-General in 1806. He was against hanging on the grounds that because courts could make mistakes, hanging was too final. He also wanted to do away with savage punishments which were not effective anyway. He managed to get Parliament to remove the death penalty for pickpocketing and some types of begging among 160 capital crimes then in existence. He felt that the certainty of being caught was more likely to deter criminals. A policeman on every street corner was the solution.

HENRY BROUGHAM (1778–1868)

Brougham was a highly intelligent and irritable man. He gave a six-hour speech in 1828 on the need for legal reforms. He got his chance to do something about improving justice when he was made Lord Chancellor (1830–4). He simplified the way cases were dealt with in the high courts, laid down new rules for the Court of Chancery and set up a new court for bankruptcy cases. He also introduced a system of paying salaries instead of fees for a number of legal officials.

15. REFORM OF THE COURTS

COUNTY COURTS ACT, 1846

There was no speedy and cheap system of bringing small civil actions. The ancient county courts could only try cases involving up to £2, and that meant little in the nineteenth century due to inflation (rising prices). To deal with the problem, an act in 1846 set up a new network of county courts 'for the more easy recovery of small debts and demands' involving up to £20 (£50 in 1850; £2,000 today). There were 59 circuits covering 500 districts. A judge would go round the courts in his circuit once a month. In the first five years of their existence, they dealt with 433,000 cases a year. The hundred courts were abolished in 1867 and the sheriff's tourns in 1887.

Trial at the Central Criminal Court (1862)

APPEALS

By the nineteenth century, the courts had developed so that their powers overlapped and their procedures had lengthened. No retrials were allowed for felony cases and rarely for those involving misdemeanours. There was no appeal from a jury's verdict or a judge's sentence unless some mistake could be found in the official court records of the case. Then a Writ of Error could be applied for. However, if a judge was in doubt as to whether the law should have allowed conviction, he could withhold his judgement until he had seen his fellow judges about the legal point in Serjeants' Inn. If the majority agreed with him, the prisoner was pardoned. In 1848 the Court of Crown Cases Reserved was set up to make this form of appeal a regular procedure. Despite this progress, there was still no way of appealing on the facts of the crime (see Court of Criminal Appeal, p.176).

JUDICATURE ACT, 1873

This act was introduced by Lord Chancellor Selborne after a long inquiry into the working of the courts. It united the Court of Appeal, which dealt with civil but not criminal appeals, and the High Court of Justice into a Supreme Court of Judicature. The High Court included the Courts of Chancery, the Probate, Divorce and Admiralty Division, and the Queen's Bench. Five judges headed the High Court's sections. New Lord Justices

---

Q1   *In the illustration above, find (a) the judge, (b) the jury, (c) the prisoner, and (d) the lawyers.*

Q2   *Draw a plan of the court marking each of them in.*

of Appeal were appointed to help these five run the Court of Appeal. It was obvious, however, that most members of the House of Lords lacked sufficient legal knowledge to hear appeals. So in 1876 new Lords of Appeal in Ordinary were appointed as 'Law Lords' in the House of Lords to hear appeals from the Court of Appeal. The reason given for not setting up a proper criminal appeal system was that a jury's verdict was expected to be accurate because it had to be unanimous.

Criminal appeals went to the Queen's Bench 'by case stated' (that is, arguing not the facts of the case, but whether a crime had been committed) instead of to the Crown Cases Reserved Court. An example in 1973 of 'by case stated' involved a dispute about a man accused of possessing cannabis leaf. He argued that the leaf was not part of the 'flowering top' banned by the Dangerous Drugs Act and therefore he had committed no offence. He lost his case.

THE DIRECTOR OF PUBLIC PROSECUTIONS, 1879

A new official was created in 1879. He was called the Director of Public Prosecutions. He and his staff were to decide whether a criminal prosecution should be brought when the police were uncertain. He would also decide what a person was to be charged with, if that was in doubt. The government's lawyer, the Attorney-General, supervised his work. This meant there was sometimes a political motive to what charges were brought, for example unlawful assembly or riot during a violent strike. The DPP can handle prosecutions himself if the matter is important to the State.

Mothers, with their children, exercising at Tothill Fields Prison

SPOTLIGHT

ELIZABETH FRY, 1780–1845

Mother of eleven children, Mrs Fry was a Quaker and wife of a London businessman. She felt it her religious duty to visit Newgate prison and found the 300 women had no privacy in their two big rooms and two cells. They were filthy and raggedly dressed, and slept with their children on the floor. She said, 'It was more like a slave-ship . . . The begging, swearing, gaming, fighting, singing, dancing . . . were too bad to be described'. From 1817 onwards she took in second-hand clothing for them and their babies and arranged for the children to be given reading and writing lessons by a prisoner. She encouraged the women to do needlework rather than be idle as she read the Bible to them. They made clothing for Botany Bay convicts: 20,000 items in the first ten months! Her Ladies' Prison Committee of a dozen friends helped her in her reforming work. She got the governor to accept specific rules for women in prison:

1. That a matron be appointed for the general superintendence of the women.

2. That women be engaged in needlework, knitting, or any other suitable employment.

3. That there be no begging, swearing, gaming or quarrelling.

4. That all novels, plays, and other improper books, be excluded.

Elizabeth Fry

5. That the women be divided into classes, of not more than twelve, and that a monitor be appointed to each class.

She inspected other prisons and did her best to persuade them to set up Ladies' Prison Committees working through the Society for the Improvement of Prison Discipline. The Society printed reports on prisons.

Q1 *For Fry, 'reform by religious emotion' was the key to success, whereas others, like J. Bentham, talked of 'reform by industry'. (a) How do you think these two methods of reform differed? (b) Which would you support and why?*

16. NINETEENTH-CENTURY PRISONS

PEEL'S GAOLS ACT, 1823

Until Robert Peel became Home Secretary in 1822, the Home Office had paid little attention to what went on in the hundreds of prisons and bridewells. Even the number of the prisons was uncertain. This is not surprising as the ministry had only 29 staff and prisons were local institutions under local control. There were no inspectors to investigate conditions or suggest reforms for the various prisons around the country. At local level JPs sometimes clashed with sheriffs over who was responsible for what went on in the prisons. In 1818, 59 prisons still did not separate males from females. Peel's Gaols Act of 1823 was a major step forward, although it only dealt with 130 prisons in London, the counties and seventeen large towns and not the hundreds of municipal or special prisons in all those towns that had a right to have a prison. It ordered JPs to run the prisons affected under the act out of the local rates. For the first time they were required to run them according to a laid down plan. This involved making sure that:

1. there was sufficient secure and sanitary accommodation;

2. the gaoler was a salaried employee of the local authority and not an independent person earning a living through the sale of favours or food;

3. prisoners submitted to a reforming discipline;

4. prisoners were properly classified; age, sex, offence, length of sentence, etc.

The JPs had to visit their prisons at least three times a quarter and report to the Quarter Sessions meetings of all the JPs. They also had to make an annual report to the Home Office. This enabled the Home Office to get information on prison conditions in Britain, and was the first step in bringing order to the confusion of the purpose-built prisons run by the local authorities, which were gradually replacing the 'private enterprise' prisons of the eighteenth century.

The pioneer work done at Gloucester Prison influenced the writing of the act. At Gloucester Prison, complete separation was rejected in favour of some association among prisoners. Men, women and children were kept apart. There were to be five classes for the purpose of work as punishment, but which class one was in depended on one's offence and not one's character. This was later regarded as a weakness of the act.

The importance of religion and education in the Gloucester system was appreciated by the planners of the act. They ordered that reading and writing were to be taught and Christian literature supplied. Moral pamphlets and Melmoth's *The Great Importance of a Religious Life* were issued. Paul's reforms on the roles of the governor, chaplain and surgeon, together with the keeping of their journals, were all to be introduced.

In practice the act was often disregarded. The small staff of five inspectors appointed by the Home Office in 1835 had a hard task in enforcing the required standards. The 200 local authorities who held the purse strings were reluctant to introduce reforms due to the cost to local ratepayers. Furthermore, the Home Secretary could not order a wrong to be put right. He could only prosecute a local authority in the courts.

Eventually the Home Office realised it had to give more precise rules about running prisons. It had two systems to choose between: (a) the Separate System; and (b) the Silent System.

THE SEPARATE SYSTEM

The 1839 Prisons Act favoured the Separate System, a system in which reform was brought about through the separation (and isolation) of prisoners. This was largely due to a report sent in by an inspector who had been impressed by Cherry Hill Penitentiary in Philadelphia during a visit to the United States. Cherry Hill Penitentiary had modelled itself on Paul's Gloucester prison system. As a result of the act, Pentonville was opened in 1842 as the government's model prison for 520 adults. It was intended that the local authorities would copy it in their prisons.

Unfortunately, the Pentonville system ignored the vital aspect about Paul's system, namely, that the total separation of prisoners from one another lasted for only the first third of a sentence, after which prisoners were brought together. At Pentonville separation was much more ruthlessly applied: it lasted the whole eighteen-month sentence. As a consequence of the enforced isolation, 22 prisoners went insane, 26 had nervous breakdowns,and three committed suicide in the first eight years after the prison was opened; a record five times worse than in other prisons. You have only to read the following details on the cells, chapel and daily routine there to see why. Not long after Pentonville's appalling record of mental torture was published, sentences at the prison were reduced to nine months.

Q1   *Compare Gloucester's system with that of Pentonville.*

Q2   *Write a newspaper article entitled, 'How the New Model Prison Treats its Inmates'.*

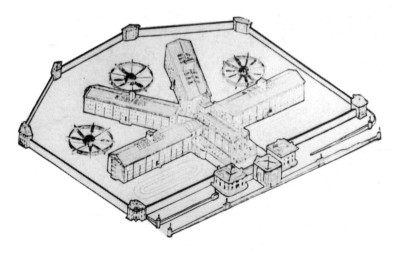

Pentonville Prison

Compare the layout of Pentonville above with Blackburn's Northleach Prison (p. 101). Each wing had 130 cells. The four funnels extracted used air as well as smoke from the heating system. There are three circular exercise yards and two rope yards in the courtyards near the entrance.

Convicts exercising in the rope yard at Pentonville

The men in the picture above are wearing grey clothes and their caps have pull-down masks with a breathing vent. The rope has knots in it every 4.5 m. Each convict grasps a knot. This keeps the prisoners apart. Then the 130 convicts are marched round at the warder's command. This exercise was to ensure they did not get constipation.

Separate cell in Pentonville Prison

The cell in the picture above measured 4.1 m by 2.3 m by 2.7 m. The size was supposed to ensure that there would be enough air for a man breathing twenty times a minute for twelve hours. The cell cost £158, which was enough at the time to build a worker's cottage. It contained a copper basin and piped water. Toilets were added too, but they have long since been removed!

Crank labour

The picture above is of Wandsworth House of Correction in 1849. When the prisoner turned the handle of the crank, a series of cups revolved and, as they came round, scooped up sand from the bottom of the box and carried it to the top of the wheel, where it was thrown out. In effect, the prisoner operated a dredger. He had to do 12,000 turns at the rate of 1,500 an hour, roughly one turn every two and a half seconds. In Leicestershire, prisoners had to do 2,000 turns to earn their breakfast and 5,000 turns to earn dinner. The handle only turned one way and the warder could reset the counter to zero from outside the cell.

Religious instruction was considered vital at Pentonville. Most prisoners liked the services held in the chapel. There were 270 cubicles arranged so that the prisoners could not see each other, but they did leave notes for each other. One cut through the floor of the chapel and got out of the prison through a ventilation shaft. Lincoln Castle in Lincolnshire contains such a chapel which is open to visitors.

Pentonville chapel

Prison chaplains played a key role in the Separate System. They visited the prisoners in their cells and stressed the point that all people were sinners who needed to be saved. Reading Prison was nicknamed 'Reading University' as its inmates learnt the New Testament by heart from morning till night. But religion was to play only a minor part in the second half of the nineteenth century. Chaplains no longer visited each prisoner regularly, but simply took services. Many people had come to the conclusion that some people were born criminals. It was argued that such people could not be reformed by any method. Phrenologists, people who claimed they could tell character by the shape of a person's head, were called in to examine prisoners and say whether they were criminal types or not. This was not so difficult as one might suspect as it was mostly convicted criminals who were examined.

A diagram used by phrenologists to point out features of the head indicating criminal behaviour

One prison surgeon said criminals had lighter brains. He argued 'Enormous jaws, high cheek bones, prominent superciliary [brows over the eyes] arches, solitary lines on the palms, extreme size of the orbits [eye-sockets], handle-shaped, or sessile [directly attached] ears' were common in criminals, savages and apes. The criminal is therefore a subspecies with congenital defects (existing from birth), he concluded.

There were at the time other just as far-fetched theories to explain criminal behaviour. Cesare Lombroso (1835–1909), a criminologist at Turin University in Italy, wrote a book called *The Criminal Man*. In it, he described features which he associated with criminal tendencies. He was particularly concerned about ears. If the lobe was missing or not easily seen, it proved a man was a criminal.

Although Pentonville had been set up as a 'model' prison and offered a well-ventilated, heated cell with toilet to slum-dweller convicts, it was a failure as a place of reform. This was a severe blow to the cause of prison reform. It had also placed heavy strain on the staff who were regularly fined for not keeping up with the routine of pressing pegs into revolving 'Tell-tale' clocks, which they had to do every fifteen minutes to prove they were on patrol. They were also banned from pubs!

Q1 *What would a modern scientist aware of evolution say about the theory held by the police surgeon?*

Q2 *List the features on the faces of Lombroso's 'criminal types' which suggest criminality to you. What sort of crimes would you say people with those features commit?*

Q3 *What do you believe a habitual criminal looks like? Do you think it is sensible to equate human features with crime?*

Q4 *Make a list of what you think was wrong with Pentonville.*

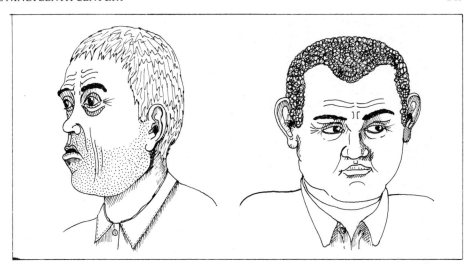

Lombroso's 'criminal types'

THE SILENT SYSTEM

If reform was impossible, then a prison like Pentonville was pointless. It was cheaper to discipline inmates in larger numbers to deter others from crime. A strict rule of silence would prevent them from communicating with each other. This idea of the Silent System came from Auburn Prison, New York, in the United States.

There were no suicides at Coldbath Fields Prison in Middlesex, but 11,624 punishments were given to 1,000 inmates in one year for trying to communicate with each other. Silent System prisons concentrated on shot drill, the treadwheel and picking oakum. Shot drill lasted for one and a quarter hours for all prisoners under 45 years old. They were lined up 2.7 m apart facing the warder. The man on one end of the line picked up a 12.6 kg cannon ball, moved sideways towards the next man, and put it down. The next man repeated the drill and in this way a stack of cannon balls was moved up and down the line. Each man moved 3.2 km during a drill. It was a tiring task, especially on hot days.

Oakum picking involved untwisting lengths of old tarred rope so that they could be used to caulk the seams of wooden ships' decks. The rope was pulled through an iron hook strapped to each convict's knees. Five hundred men could do this job in a single room. It was a very dusty job.

Those on hard labour did from 1.3 to 2.7 kg a day, while boys under 16 years old did 0.7 kg and girls, 0.5 kg. The prison did 3,556 kg a week, and sold the untwisted rope to the Royal Navy and ship owners.

Q1 *How might prisoners on silence try to communicate with each other?*

Part of the large oakum room at Middlesex House of Correction, Coldheath Fields Prison, under the Silent System

Gradually statistics began to show that neither the Separate nor the Silent System lowered the recommittal rate (rate at which ex-prisoners returned to prison). Prisons of the nineteenth century seemed to do little more than keep their inmates off the streets. This proved a great disappointment to many who had really hoped to reform prisoners. There seemed no alternative but to deter people by harsh methods.

PRISON ACTS

Prisons Act, 1865: 'Hard labour, hard fare and a hard board'

The alternative to the Separate and Silent Systems that had attempted to reform prisoners was one of harshness designed to frighten convicts from committing crimes when released and, at the same time, scaring all potential offenders from crime. The aim of the Prison Act of 1865 was to enforce a strict, uniform regime of punishment on all 193 local prisons, but not to try to reform prisoners through work or religion.

The act allowed for:

1. Separation or cellular confinement for nine months;

2. Hard Labour, 1st Class, for a minimum of three months to include treadwheel, crank, capstan, shot drill, stonebreaking, oakum picking; Hard Labour, 2nd Class, to include less strenuous tasks;

3. Putting prisoners in close confinement for three days on bread and water on the governor's orders (visiting Justices could increase this to a month and add a whipping); the use of irons;

Q1 *Compare and contrast the Separate and Silent Systems.*

Q2 *Explain 'Hard labour, hard fare and hard board'. Give examples of each.*

CLASS 3

Convicted Prisoners employed at hard labour for terms exceeding fourteen days, but not more than six weeks; and convicted Prisoners not employed at hard labour for terms exceeding fourteen days, and not more than three months.

BREAKFAST

Males	*Females*
1 pint of Oatmeal Gruel.	1 pint of Oatmeal Gruel.
8 ounces of Bread.	6 ounces of Bread.

DINNER

Sunday and Thursday

1 pint of Soup.	1 pint of Soup.
8 ounces of Bread.	6 ounces of Bread.

Tuesday and Saturday

3 ounces of cooked Meat,	3 ounces of cooked Meat,
without bone.	without bone.
8 ounces of Bread.	6 ounces of Bread.
½ lb. of Potatoes.	½ lb. of Potatoes.

Monday, Wednesday and Friday

8 ounces of Bread.	6 ounces of Bread.
1 lb. of Potatoes, or 1 pint	1 lb. of Potatoes, or 1 pint
of Gruel when Potatoes	of Gruel when Potatoes
cannot be obtained.	cannot be obtained.

SUPPER

Same as Breakfast.	Same as Breakfast.

Hard labour diet at Gloucester Prison

4. Replacing of hammocks with board beds;

5. Abolishing the distinction between gaols and houses of correction. Some 80 small prisons closed down rather than face the cost and problems involved. But the Home Office's control over the remaining 113 prisons was not easy. If an Inspector reported deficiencies, the Home Secretary had to contact the local JPs and if they would not act, prosecute them in the courts. Also some city prisons remained overcrowded while other country ones were underused.

Prisons Act, 1877

The new act twelve years later had three major effects.

1. Local prisons were 'nationalised' so that they came under Home Office control alongside the government's convict prisons. Local authorities would not spend money on them and the government had promised a rates' reduction, so the solution was to let the general taxpayer pay.

2. Fifty-three prisons were closed. Wales, with its reputation for a low crime rate, lost Anglesey, Brecon (restored 1881), Cardiganshire, Flintshire, Merionethshire, Montgomeryshire and Radnorshire Prisons.

3. A three-man Prison Commission was set up to run all the prisons in England and Wales.

County Gaol staff, Caernarvon, c. 1892

One Law for the Rich and Another for the Poor?

In 1866 the Howard Association started with the intention of keeping a close eye on the prison system and the handling of criminals. In 1921 it merged with the Prison Reform League to become the Howard League for Penal Reform. Here are two cases in two centuries which it noted as evidence of unequal justice.

Case One, 1876: 'A poor motherless boy, of only 7 years of age, was charged with rolling in a barley field'. The weeping boy was fined and sent to prison. The Howard Association asked 'How about the royal railway carriage stoned near Eton College not long ago? Did any noble youth suffer imprisonment then?'

Case Two, 1975: Two seventeen-year-olds were jailed for four years for starting fires which caused £18,000 damage to a primary school; the Durham Crown Court judge said, 'School arson has to be stamped out'. The same week, an eighteen-year-old second cousin to the Queen was conditionally discharged for setting fire to his bedroom at Harrow School and doing £92,000 damage; the Old Bailey judge said, 'To send you to prison or to a borstal institution would serve no useful purpose.'

Q1 *On the face of it these contrasting judgements in both cases seem very unfair; what factors might explain the difference in the administering of justices apart from the class backgrounds of those involved?*

CHAPTER 8

The Twentieth Century – Part 1

---

1. THE POLICE

It could be said that a man or woman travelling from the nineteenth century into the twentieth century in a time machine would have little difficulty in recognising a British court of law. Methods of charging and trying criminals have not altered dramatically in the last 85 to 90 years. True, capital punishment has been abandoned; legal aid, the right of appeal on criminal cases, the right of non-property owners to serve as jurors, and a host of other reforms, have been introduced. But basically the system of justice has not altered out of all recognition since the turn of the century. Methods of law enforcement by the police, on the other hand, have changed markedly during the twentieth century. Although the nineteenth-century police had become professional within the bounds of nineteenth-century technology, the twentieth century has witnessed cosiderable progress in the training and resources available to police officers.

POLICE TRAINING
Let us look briefly at the types of police and the training the modern British policeman or policewoman enjoys.

Police Cadets
Youths of both sexes from sixteen to eighteen years of age may join the Police Cadets, although not all forces in the country have facilities to run Cadet Forces. They wear the same unform as adult police except for a 'CADET' shoulder flash and a pale blue band round their caps. They work alongside the police and get experience in community work as well as adventure training.

The Police

The normal age for direct entry into the police is eighteen or nineteen. Recruits have to be 1.73 m tall for men and 1.62 m for women. They have to be healthy and honest, as well as prepared to accept discipline and able to show common sense and initiative. Black or Asian candidates are given advice to help them with language tests if they need it. They will all have a fourteen-week residential course at a Police Training Centre (Metropolitan Police do twenty weeks at Hendon Centre). Women police started in 1920.

The modern policewoman

A policewoman enforcing the ban against nude bathing in the Serpentine in London's Hyde Park over 50 years ago

Some of the things recruits have to learn are: (a) how to control traffic; (b) how to warn and arrest people; (c) how to give evidence in court; (d) how to deal with an accident, including measuring skid marks, interviewing witnesses, etc.; (e) the law itself.

Q1 *Devise and carry out a practical lesson for a new recruit on one of (a)–(e). Video it if possible.*

Graduate Entry

Graduate Entry is open to degree holders under 30 years old who are likely to gain high promotion. Interviews and tests last $2\frac{1}{2}$ days as only 25 to 30 people are accepted each year. Successful applicants do a Special Course at the Police Staff College, Bramshill, Hants (founded 1948). They will be inspectors within six years of finishing the special course.

'Special' Constables

'Special' constables, part-time police, have been employed since 1923.

Traffic Wardens

Traffic wardens now save the police a lot of time and release them for more important policing tasks by handling many traffic matters.

Five Reasons Why the Policeman's and Policewoman's Role is Difficult

1. The kinds of person their work makes them. Confrontation with criminals and crime may make them angry in the way they work or make them believe the worst of others.

2. They have to maintain their authority which may tempt them to overreact when provoked.

3. If they get too friendly with people they may find it difficult to arrest them if the need arises.

4. To get promotion and avoid being told off they must produce results. So they may be tempted to make arrests for the sake of arrests.

5. They may have prejudices against particular criminals or crimes. This may make their way of applying the law uneven.

Police Resources and Their Uses

TV programmes regularly suggest that fast police cars backed up by radio control are the solution to crime. In fact the public are the best crime preventers. If they lock their houses securely and fix devices to their windows, and do not leave tempting belongings in cars, stealing is more

Q1 *Find out how the uniforms of 'Special' constables differ and what these constables usually do.*

Q2 *Describe a situation to fit each of the five points in the box above and explain what would be the right or wrong thing for the PC or WPC to do.*

EXAMPLES OF POLICE SPECIALISATION

River Police, 1798
Motor boats, 1910.
Cover 54 miles of
R. Thames

*Sciences of Crime
Officers (SOCO)*
Take fingerprints, take
footprint castings,
photograph the scene
and search for evidence.

*Special Patrol Group
(SPG)*
Consists of eight units of
34 men. To cope with any
major emergency.

*Community Relations
Branch, 1968*
Community Liaison
Officers' job is to improve
relations between the
police and the
community, supervise
Juvenile Bureau, etc.

Dog Handling
1914, owner PCs may
take their dogs on the
beat. 1946, regular
system set up. Today
there are 300 dogs in use
in London.

Air Support Unit, 1980
In 1921 used borrowed
airship to watch crowd
and traffic at the Derby.
Today traffic helicopters
make regular runs over
London. They have TV
cameras, searchlights
and public address
system.

Organised Crimes Squad
'Gangbusters'.

Drugs Squad
To catch drug dealers
and smugglers.

Regional Crime Squads
They link up work
between different forces.
In 1967, 170 forces were
reduced to 43 in England
and Wales.

Mounted Police, 1758
Today horses between
three and eighteen years
old and sixteen hands
high are used. They are
ridden for three hours a
day.

Forensic Scientists
First laboratory, Hendon,
1934–5. National
Fingerprint Office.
Fingerprinting began in
1860; full system, 1901.

Murder Squad
Cope with murder cases.

*Crime Prevention
Department*
To alert the public on the
need to prevent crime
and how to do it.

Central Robbery Squad
Originally the 'Flying
Squad', 1919, named
after ex-Royal Flying
Corps vehicles it used.

*Criminal Investigation
Department (CID)*
Special detective work.

Special Branch
Began 1883, as special
team against Irish
terrorists.

*Anti-Terrorist Squad,
1971*
Began as the Bomb
Squad against the Angry
Brigade.

difficult. Because the 'bobby on the beat' regularly patrolling the same area becomes the friend of those who live and work there, this encourages citizens to inform and aid him. Known as the Home Beat Officer, he or she will also be more likely to spot something unusual than the driver of a patrol car who has to watch which way he or she is steering.

Q1   *Find out who your Home Beat Officer is and the area he or she covers. What are the main problems that area presents?*

Q2   *If you were a police patrol person and came upon a road accident, list in the correct order all the things you would have to do. Show your list to a policeman or policewoman and see what he or she thinks of your list.*

The Home Beat Officer at work

POLICE RESOURCES

SPOTLIGHT

SPOTLIGHT

COMMUNICATION
Telephone, first used 1901. 1934, public told to dial 'Whitehall 1212'; 1937, to dial '999'.

Radio, introduced in 1910. First used to arrest the murderer, Dr Crippen.

Two-way radio, introduced in 1922–3. 1932, pocket-sets issued.

Police National Computer, Hendon On stolen vehicles, criminals' records, wanted and missing persons, fingerprint records. Metropolitan Police Computer, 1984, controls 1,000 sets of traffic lights and handling of '999' calls.

Closed-circuit TV 'Hoolivan' with TV camera on roof, introduced 1985.

SPEED
Horses, introduced 1758.

Rowing and sailing boats, introduced 1798.

Bikes, introduced 1909.

Motorboats, introduced 1910.

Cars, introduced 1919.

Motorbikes, introduced 1930s.

Helicopters, introduced 1970s.

Q1 *How does the '999' system work?*

The arrest of Dr Crippen on board the liner
Montrose, *made possible by the use of wireless*
messages between the captain and Scotland Yard

SHOULD THESE RESOURCES BE USED BY THE POLICE?

The introduction of new technology to combat crime is sometimes
regarded with alarm by the public. Their worry is that the methods used
to catch criminals may be used to invade the privacy of innocent citizens
or used by a government to check on a person's ideas or opinions. A free
society must be careful to maintain a balance between the individual's
freedom and the need for society to protect itself against criminal
elements. Let us look at two examples on which arguments arise.

1. Interception of mail and telephone calls

Intercepting the mail of suspicious characters was efficiently done for the
government between 1716 and 1844 by generations of the Willes family
working in London's main post office. The Revd E. Willes (active 1716–43)
was promoted in the Church each time he uncovered a Jacobite plot.
Eventually their work was discovered and halted. In the 1980s, it came to
light that letters and telephones of people belonging to trade unions, the
Campaign for Nuclear Disarmament (CND), and other organisations were
probably being interfered with. The European Court of Human Rights
ruled against the government's handling of these interceptions. The
government stressed that a minister's warrant had to be issued for this to
be done, but many MPs felt that ministers had lost control of what was
going on. Consequently a tribunal was set up in 1985 to award people
unlimited damages if their mail or telephone calls were intercepted
without proper authorisation.

2. Use of firearms

From 1976 to 1980, five deaths and six injuries were caused by police using firearms. In 1981, 11,486 issues of firearms were authorised; 39 shots were fired, of which 36 were to destroy dangerous animals. In 1983 two detective constables were acquitted of seriously wounding Stephen Waldorf, thought by them to be a man wanted for shooting at a policeman, when his Mini stopped in a London traffic jam. DC Finch said he thought the man was about to draw a gun. He hit him on the head after DC Jardine had also shot Mr Waldorf. The prosecution produced no evidence that they had intended to kill or injure Mr Waldorf. In law the two were correctly acquitted, but fear was expressed that there was a danger of police shooting people without risk of being charged so long as they believed, however mistakenly, that they themselves were in danger. Although the two DCs had committed no offence in law, doubt remained as to whether they had lived up to their training and kept the rules on gun handling. The case left the police worried about whether they should or should not use guns again in such circumstances.

COMPLAINTS AGAINST THE POLICE

Most people would agree that the citizens of a free country have the right to bring complaints against the police for inefficiency, insulting behaviour, disregard for public safety, or illegal actions. The difficult thing to agree on is how those complaints should be made and what group should investigate the complaints. One of the problems is that the police currently investigate complaints against themselves. There is no board of inquiry totally independent of the police to do the job. A complaint will first be investigated by a senior officer, if necessary from another force. If he cannot resolve it, it will go to the Police Complaints Authority (PCA). Until 1985 this was known as the Police Complaints Board (PCB).

In 1982 the PCB said it 'was satisfied that in the vast majority of cases . . . a thorough and fair investigation has been made.' Almost all complaints imply that a PC has committed a disciplinary offence as a policeman and so his action will automatically be investigated.

In April 1985 the PCA began work. Its three-member tribunals include a retired policeman from the ranks of the accused's staff association. A QC chairs its meetings. The PCA expects to hear about 200 major cases a year involving complaints connected with death, serious injuries or corruption, or any other case it considers is in the public interest. It leaves the

---

Q1   *List the arguments for and against arming the police. Hold a discussion and vote on whether policemen should carry guns, and if so, under what circumstances.*

Q2   *List possible minor and major incidents of police handling of a person or situation which would give rise to complaints.*

yearly average of 3,000 minor cases to be investigated by individual forces. Any policeman who loses his job or is demoted has the right to legal representation before the PCA.

CAN THE POLICE COPE?

A study in London a few years ago showed that for every 100 burglaries reported a further 37 were not. Is the public co-operating fully with the police in reporting crimes? Many think it is not. Many others think the public is ignoring warnings from the police and not showing sufficient interest in self-help policing. They believe that crime prevention by the public is the best answer to the growth of crime.

There is now a Crime Prevention Centre at Stafford in Staffordshire to train police to help the public help themselves. Police forces have a range of leaflets for protecting houses, cars, caravans and boats against theft, and for 'Good Neighbour Schemes' – for example, helping those away on holiday by borrowing their key and 'looking in'.

Poster for a 'Good Neighbour Scheme'

A warning to the public

Today, private companies like Securicor, public groups and invididuals are lending their assistance to the police in the battle against crime. Vehicles to carry payrolls, shop receipts and money between banks are now a common sight. In 1985 one a day was attacked compared to one a month in 1975. This has led to cameras being fitted to the vehicles. An organisation called 'Nightwatch' appeared in Winchester as a private anti-crime force in 1985. Its members, who wore white helmets and jackets and carried radios but no weapons, patrolled the streets from 11 p.m. to 6 a.m. In Winchester 80 firms and shops promptly contributed £1 a night for the service. The local police said they welcomed the help. The scheme was launched in Winchester to commemorate the Statute of Winchester, 1285. A year later, due to public lack of interest, 'Nightwatch' was disbanded in Winchester.

White-suited private guards who patrolled Winchester in 1985–6 to deter crime

Every citizen has still got the right of Citizen's Arrest, that is, to arrest anyone he or she sees committing a crime. It is a citizen's duty, in fact. In 1984–5, George Anderson, 46, an unemployed painter, made 31 such arrests of shoplifters in Lincoln. 'I feel I am fulfilling a public need', he said. 'I pass the evidence to the police and they prosecute.'

Q1 *What did that Statute of Winchester, 1285, provide for? What connection can you find between it and 'Nightwatch'?*

2. CRIMINALS AND VICTIMS

Courts can order offenders to pay compensation to victims. Since 1982, an offender too poor to pay both a fine and compensation pays compensation first. Since 1964 the Criminal Injuries Compensation Board in London has given financial help to people injured as a result of a crime, trying to stop a criminal or helping the police. Requests can only be dealt with if at least £400 would be a fair compensation. Compensation covers pain, loss of earnings, or injury to self or property. In 1974 the National Association of Victims Support Schemes began in Bristol. Now 170 towns have similar schemes. Volunteers can be of any age and are given training. The police arrange for volunteers to call on victims. Volunteers help to calm those who are upset, contact insurance firms and fit new locks, etc.

Some schemes for direct reparation are beginning. These involve the offender making a direct payment or providing a service (repair of the damage done) to the victim. The victim must agree before direct reparation can take place.

TWENTIETH-CENTURY CRIME

Our century has seen the introduction of new crimes and old crimes with new names.

Some Twentieth-century Crimes

Mugging
Assaults with attempts to rob.

Computer Crimes
Discovering a computer code and using it to transfer money to your use.

The Sit-in
People occupying a factory which is to be closed, taking over a forces missile base, etc.

Vandalism, Hooliganism
Damage to telephone kiosks, park seats; graffiti on walls. Fighting, rioting at football matches, etc.

Turning Back Car Mileometer
In 1981 one garage owner was fined £500 for 24 offences, but he made £500 per car more from this crime.

Traffic Offences
Speeding, not stopping at junctions, illegal parking, dangerous driving, drunken driving, etc.

Racial Crimes
Tormenting and threatening of minority groups and committing attacks on their property.

Smuggling by Air
Smuggling drugs through airports or by private aircraft owners.

Q1   *Has your town got such a victim support scheme? Do they still need volunteers?*

Q2   *Discuss the crimes in the table. Produce examples of each. How are they dealt with and what kind of punishments are given? What other twentieth-century crimes can you think of?*

Smuggling

Watch smuggling started up in Britain after 1945 when watches had $33\frac{1}{3}$ per cent duty and only 2 million were allowed in each year. Smugglers brought in 500 to 5,000 per trip using double-lined cases, waistcoats and body belts. In 1950 Mrs Noreen Harbord's Chrysler had 7,742 watches hidden behind the upholstery, in hollow parts of the chassis, and in a dummy battery case. The haul was worth £30,000. She denied all knowledge, the car was confiscated and she was released. Unbeknown to her, the police observed her movements. When she contacted two racing drivers, one had his car stopped at Newhaven with 3,000 watches in the petrol tank. The two drivers were arrested. It was discovered that the pair normally made 40 journeys a year. They and Mrs Harbord were all jailed. When the duty was cancelled and the import restriction removed, the smuggling of watches ended.

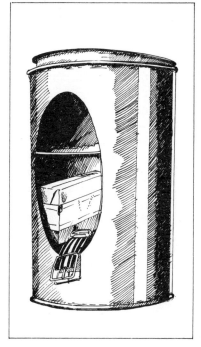

False-bottomed tin for smuggling drugs
A smuggler's waistcoat with watches hung internally

The smuggling of Pakistanis, Indians and Cypriots took place in the 1960s. They were ferried over from France or Belgium. One fisherman got five years in prison for smuggling in 200 illegal immigrants.

Drug smuggling is now a major problem. It has been smuggled as mango pickles, tins of jam and inside children's hollow toys. Airports have a major problem trying to catch the smugglers. X-ray machines and sniffer dogs are now used.

Shoplifting
What is your image of an average shoplifter? See if you are right after reading on.

Shoplifting has doubled in each decade since 1960. In Plymouth in 1976, 417 persons were convicted: 218 males; 199 females. Of those convicted, 152 were under 29 years old; 98 were 50 or more years old; strangely 222 had more money on them than the stolen items cost. Finally, 213 were first offenders. The conclusions from this study were : (a) shoplifters were local adults who stole from large stores because they were greedy, although a large minority did have money or health problems; (b) 'shop lifting is theft' notices seemed to encourage juveniles to do it for bravado; (c) young poor mothers stole food and household goods, while alcoholic men stole to get drink; (d) middle-aged women account for 5 to 10 per cent of shoplifters, and they may steal to protest at their family's thankless demands or neglect by loved ones; (e) foreign holiday-makers have figured as shoplifters in London.

White-collar Crimes
Fraud, tax evasion, computer manipulation, failure to maintain safety and health standards in factories, restaurants and hotels, etc., can all be called 'white-collar crimes'. In fact there are many more convictions of working-class or unemployed people for fraudulent social security claims than there are of middle-class swindlers. Although tax avoidance is not a crime while tax evasion is, tax evasion may be aided by accountants advising clients how to *avoid* paying taxes. Computer crimes need high intelligence and persistence and are not easily detectable. They can bring big profits too. In spite of factory and health inspectors, etc., a few firms continue to leave machinery unprotected or kitchens in filthy conditions. It is thought that such crimes persist because of a lack of inspectors. Most firms and restaurants are visited once every four years unless a violation has been committed. Such inspectors do not see themselves as 'an industrial police force'; they tend to warn and return repeatedly rather than prosecute.

Q1 *What changes in shop designs since the 1960s have encouraged shoplifting?*

Q2 *What would you do if you saw someone shoplifting?*

Q3 *What is a 'store detective' and who employs him or her?*

Q4 *Why does society not get worked up over white-collar crime?*

Q5 *Are white-collar crimes rightly named?*

COMMENTS ON TWENTIETH-CENTURY CRIME

It is easy to jump to the wrong conclusions when reading crime statistics. Some 680 murders occurred in 1980. This looks alarming, but in fact the number included 47 people who died in two London arson cases. This was the first year that such murders were included in the figures. The fact that immigrants tend to live in poor areas where the crime rate is higher does not mean that they commit the crimes. In fact it is more likely to be the local native population.

Occasionally the law is changed and new crimes are listed. But the reverse is also true. Suicide was a crime from 1854 to 1961.

Robbery and break-in have increased much more than other crimes since World War II. *Burglary* means entering a building illegally with intent to commit a crime. *Robbery* means taking someone's property by violence or with a threat of violence. *Theft* means taking someone's property.

3. LAW AND ORDER IN THE TWENTIETH CENTURY

The struggle to control mass demonstrations and rioting continues. Trade union picketing has been the scene of such serious conflicts that there is a question of whether 'policing by consent' is possible in such circumstances.

TONYPANDY, 1910

Local JPs called for troops when miners rioted in the Rhondda Valley at Tonypandy in 1910. The chief constable told Home Secretary Winston Churchill that the position was grave. Churchill replied:

> 'Your request for military. Infantry should not be used till all other means have failed. Following arrangements have therefore been made. Seventy

---

Q1 *Some crimes have a high media visibility (that is, they are crimes which make headlines) while others have a low media visibility. List three crimes under these headings: (a) high; (b) low; (c) variable visibility. Why are some crimes variable?*

Q2 *What difference would the law make to someone who failed in a suicide attempt in 1960 compared with one who failed in 1962?*

Q3 *Does the fact that criminals who are caught tend to be poor and ill-educated with unstable job records prove that such people are normally criminals? Or does it simply prove that they are the type of criminals who get caught most?*

Q4 *Answer the following questions: (a) Do you think this increase in robbery and break-in shows that people are getting more careless with their property as they have got more prosperous? (b) Are such crimes due to a way of life which emphasises material prosperity?*

mounted constables [in fact, 100 were sent] and two hundred foot constables of Metropolitan Police will come to Pontypridd by special train leaving Paddington 4.55 p.m., arriving about 8.0 p.m. They will carry out your directions under their own officers. The County will bear the cost. Expect these forces will be sufficient, but as further precautionary measure 200 cavalry will be moved into the district tonight and remain there pending cessation [waiting for the end] of trouble. Infantry meanwhile will be at Swindon. General Macready will command the military and will act in conjunction with the civil authorities as circumstances may require. The military will not, however, be available unless it is clear that the police reinforcements are unable to cope with the situation. Telegraph news Home Office and say whether these arrangements are sufficient.'

In fact baton charges proved sufficient and the troops beat the miners in a football match.

LIVERPOOL'S 'BLOODY SUNDAY', 15 AUGUST 1911

Liverpool dockers were taking part in an orderly march when some hooligans started a fight with the police. Baton charges failed and a 'cavalry charge' of 30 mounted police with staves followed. One policeman was kicked to death and a free-for-all followed. The Riot Act was read and the mob dispersed, leaving two dead. A nationwide railway strike followed. Churchill put troops on the alert over a wide area. In Chesterfield troops made a bayonet charge and in Llanelli they opened fire and killed two people. In fact hooligans rather than strikers were largely to blame. Churchill was criticised for allowing troops to go into action without JPs' requests, but it was argued that troops had as much right as citizens to keep law and order. When there were 1 million people on strike in 1912, the leaders sent a leaflet to soldiers, saying: 'You are Working men's Sons. *You* are called upon by your officers to *Murder Us* . . . Boys. Don't Do It.' The authors received brief sentences under the 1797 Incitement to Mutiny Act.

SUFFRAGETTES, 1910–14

Window smashing, pillar-box arson, bombing and the disruption of meetings and church services became the hallmarks of the women's campaign for votes before World War I. Women chained themselves to fences and Emily Davison, an Oxford graduate with a 1st Class degree, died in her attempt to disrupt the Derby. 'Black Friday', 18 November, 1910, saw a severe clash in Parliament Square. The women complained that their hair was pulled, their clothes torn and that they were punched and kicked. Their offences and the harsh treatment they received in prison will be examined on pp. 199–203.

Q1   *Is violence ever justified for any cause?*

The arrest of a Suffragette, May 1914

Manchester police with their new Gladstone shields, 1913

THE GENERAL STRIKE, 1926

The Emergency Powers Act of 1920 was used when miners, transport workers and many other workers went on strike in 1926. The government argued that the Trades Union Congress (TUC) was trying to overthrow the British system of government, although this was strenuously denied. The strike committee insisted on no violence and football was played with the police. But 140,000 'specials' were sworn in and a lorry load of chair legs issued as truncheons. Some vehicles were overturned and a train derailed but it was to the credit of all that no real fighting occurred.

The General Strike, 1926. Police escort buses as a soldier looks on.

The General Strike, 1926. Police v. Strikers at football. The two teams pose before the match at which the wife of the Chief Constable of Plymouth kicked off.

Mounted Special Constables, 1926

FLYING PICKETS AND THE SPECIAL PATROL GROUP, 1972

In 1972 'flying pickets' added a new problem to strike control. Coach loads of building workers used the motorways to intimidate those who would not strike. Motorways now provide an alternative to railways for troublemakers to use. The trial of the 'Shrewsbury Six' for conspiring to disrupt work on six building sites showed just how thin the line between peaceful and illegal picketing was, and how the police were caught in the middle of conflict between the right to demonstrate and the right to work. Three of the 'flying pickets' were sent to prison and three acquitted. They claimed their trial was a political one against the right to demonstrate. In 1974–5 the fear that parliamentary government might collapse led to the start of some unofficial organisations ready to maintain law and order if the breakdown occurred. One organisation, 'GB 75' created by retired army officers, planned to ensure factories kept going by ejecting strikers and getting workers in by helicopters.

THE MARCH ON LONDON'S RED LION SQUARE, 1974

On 15 June 1974, a Communist march entered London's Red Lion Square, and some of its members charged the police, using the sharpened ends of their banner poles as pikes. Special Patrol Group men retaliated, using the tactic of a wedge-shaped charge to split the demonstrators into two groups. Heavy fighting followed as a National Front procession arrived to add to the confusion. One demonstrator died and others were injured, including 39 policemen. A *Riot Control* booklet published in 1975 by the Royal United Services Institute for Defence Studies listed the weapons which might have to be used if there was a danger of the breakdown of law and order. They included electrified water jets, barbed contacts, dart guns, rubber bullets and sound curdlers. Although the Metropolitan Police acquired water cannon in the 1980s, they have not used them because the jets of water can hurl debris from the ground at people and seriously injure them.

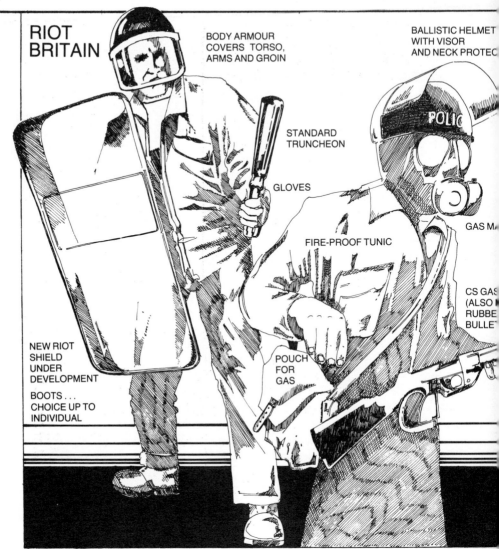

RIOT
BRITAIN

BODY ARMOUR
COVERS TORSO,
ARMS AND GROIN

BALLISTIC HELMET
WITH VISOR
AND NECK PROTEC

POLIC

STANDARD
TRUNCHEON

GLOVES

GAS M

FIRE-PROOF TUNIC

CS GAS
(ALSO
RUBBE
BULLE

NEW RIOT
SHIELD
UNDER
DEVELOPMENT

POUCH
FOR
GAS

BOOTS...
CHOICE UP TO
INDIVIDUAL

'Positive' policing in a riot means new-look bobbies and sophisticated control tac

The traditional image of the British bobby succumbed this week to the unprecedented viciousness of rioters using such missiles as petrol bombs modified to act like napalm (writes Maris Ross).

With more than 350 policemen injured while wearing ordinary uniform, Home Secretary William Whitelaw immediately authorised crash-type headgear and fireproof overalls for riot duty, with CS gas as a last resort.

These are only the first of changes which James Jardine, Chairman of the Police Federation (the trade union for lower ranking policemen), reluctantly believes are necessary 'because we are moving into a new era.'

As the bobbies' representative, he is asking Mr Whitelaw for rubber bullets, water cannon, body armour, better shields, protected vehicles with shatterproof glass arc lights for night disturbances and fire extinguishers.

An article from The Observer, *12 July, 1981, shows the depth of feeling that arises from police anti-riot techniques*

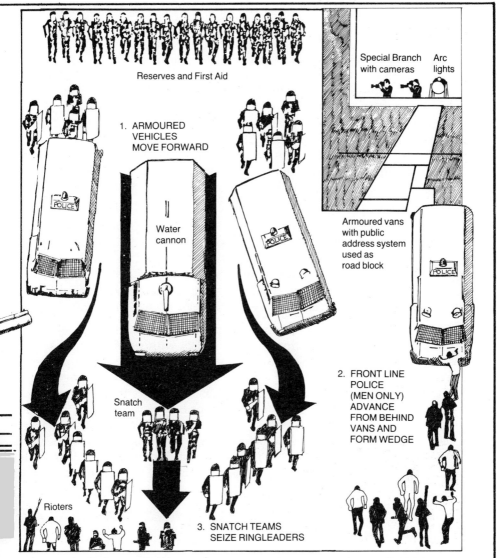

These would be coupled with better training and advice from the Royal Ulster Constabulary and foreign police on their tactics to contain rioters, split them into ineffective groups and literally 'snatch' ringleaders.

'We're fed up with being aunt sallies, standing there and taking it,' Mr Jardine said. 'One of the reasons we're asking for positive policing is because while we're standing still, they've got time to collect missiles in piles.'

Mr Jardine is well aware public opinion might not countenance rubber bullets and water cannon.

'The last thing I wanted was to change the image of the police force. We've always been known as the best and friendliest police force in the world. Nobody's tried harder to preserve that in the face of terrible injuries. It breaks our hearts that the traditional look of the policeman is gone now.'

Q1 *Is the newspaper article in favour of or against the introduction of 'positive' policing?*

RIOTS AT TOXTETH IN LIVERPOOL AND BRIXTON IN LONDON, 1981

As political rioting declined, rioting started to break out in some deprived inner cities. Unemployment (around 40 per cent in Toxteth), poor housing and racial tensions led to mass destruction and petrol bombing. The then Home Secretary William Whitelaw promised that the police would get better protective headgear and fire-resistant clothing. He supported the first use of the incapacitating CS gas in England at Toxteth against 30 rioting youngsters. CS gas had been available since the mid-1960s. One girl of thirteen years was charged with arson and another of fifteen with assaulting a policeman. 'Policing by consent' seemed at an end in the face of white and black youths and girls destroying whatever was in reach.

Some people did not agree that the riots were caused by economic hardship. The desire of youths for possessions and 'being somebody' existed before the riots. For some years a quarter of Liverpool's criminals had been below sixteen years of age. Supporters of firmer police action blamed the riots on the belief some people had that they had a 'right to the good things in life', whether they had earned them or not.

Serious thought was given to how to police deprived and racially tense areas after these riots. 'Community Policing', with its old-fashioned foot patrols, was to replace the use of 'panda' cars. (Each 1 per cent increase in police presence has produced a 1 per cent increase in crime detection.) Lord Scarman in a famous report issued after the Brixton Riots recommended that police liaison committees be formed to bring the police and communities together. However, in August 1985, youths attacked police in Toxteth on several occasions so that the chief constable said he was concerned about being able to continue foot patrols. Meanwhile, arson attacks against Asians continue to cause the loss of innocent lives and to increase racial tension.

SPOTLIGHT

FOOTBALL HOOLIGANISM, 1923–85

The sight of police escorting trains and coach loads of supporters carrying beer cans on their way to football matches has become common. 'Hooligan' refers to the name of a London family involved in the serious August Bank Holiday rioting in 1898. Football hooliganism is nothing new. Before World War I, soldiers and sailors were let in free so that they could help the police against rioting youths. The first Wembley Cup Final in 1923 between Bolton Wanderers and West Ham was a near disaster when up to an estimated 300,000 crowded into the new stadium built for 125,000. Those with tickets could not reach their seats and spectators swarmed onto the pitch. PC George Storey, on a massive white horse, took 40 minutes to quietly herd the fans on the pitch back to their seats, although they again spilled onto the pitch during the game. Twenty-four out of the 1,000 injured were taken to hospital. In 1946, 33 fans died when a wall broke under crowd pressure at Bolton's stadium.

The behaviour of fans (and often players!) has spoilt many games. Closed-circuit TV manned by police to spot and identify trouble-makers, high protective fencing, identity cards, a ban on beer and other remedies have been suggested. But who are behind the troubles? Evidence shows it is not the unemployed teenager but organised gangs of well-off, upper- and middle-class men between 18 and 25 years of age, often married, and paying mortgages on their houses. Chelsea's Anti-Personnel Firm, a notoriously tough gang found at Chelsea's games at home and away, come from the rich London suburbs and dress in clothes from upmarket shops. They leave their victims with gold-embossed calling cards, announcing: 'Nothing Personal! – You Have Been Serviced by the Anti-Personnel Firm.' They are amused that Manchester City's Main Line Service Crew, another gang of football hooligans, still proudly identify themselves by labels on their *Pringle* sweaters. Main Line's 'general' got five-years' imprisonment in 1985.

In the 1970s violence occurred on the terraces, but the new gangs sit in the expensive seats. In March 1985, the seats that Millwall's Half-Way Liners threw at the police cost them £10 each to sit on. As they can afford to arrive in cars, they avoid the police escorts and sit where they like. They use CB radios to converge on other teams' supporters' coaches across London. Leicester City's Baby Squad are all still at school, wear 'Wham!' T-shirts and carry Stanley knives. West Ham's Inter-City Firm (they use Inter-City trains instead of football specials) has black members on equal terms with white in its 400 strong membership. Membership of these gangs is like belonging to a tribe and gives life a meaning for its members. Punishing them will not necessarily solve the problem. It may simply provide hooligans with martyrs or heroes. The solution must lie in providing them with an alternative *meaning* to life which is sufficiently tempting. Boredom and frustration often lie behind their actions. Their desire for glory makes them see a fight as a glorious achievement. In fact most fights occur off the football grounds and this will only increase if the clamp-down in the grounds is tighter.

Q1 *What common factors can you find behind teenage trouble in Toxteth, Brixton and football hooliganism?*

Q2 *If you were a chief constable how would you tackle: (a) an inner-city riot; (b) football hooliganism; (c) an invasion of Hell's Angels?*

West Ham Supporters arrive at Wembley for the 1923 Cup Final match against Bolton Wanderers

Over 300,000 fans crowded into a Wembley which had seating for 125,000 in the 1923 Cup Final

Q1   Compare the clothing and the age of these 1923 football supporters in the pictures above with those of today. What difference is there in their expressions which suggests there will be no violence such as today's hooligans get up to?

Q2   What in your view is the cause of riots in Britain's inner cities?

THE MINERS' STRIKE, 1984

This long and serious strike forced chief constables throughout the country (who behaved like 'medieval warlords' with their militias, claimed one miner's defence solicitor) to help each other out by loans of detachments of police to areas outside their own. The considerable overtime payments paid to the police and the way they beat a tattoo on their riot shields annoyed the strikers. Things came to a head at Orgreave coking plant on June 18. After riot and unlawful assembly charges were dropped by the prosecution against 79 strikers, their defence solicitor said that 8,000 police had deliberately shepherded the strikers into a field and then mounted police made a 'cavalry' charge into them. She maintained that the official police film made of all that happened that day showed the 'infantry' dressed in 'strange medieval battle dress with helmets and visors, round shields and overalls . . . run after the cavalry and begin truncheoning the pickets'. The film showed that the pickets began to throw missiles after the charges. The defence solicitor claimed that the TV news had reversed the events by showing the missile throwing before the charges.

GREENHAM COMMON

A quite different problem facing the police today is that posed by peace groups at nuclear missile sites such as Greenham Common. On the whole this has involved little more than the good-natured picking up of people sitting down in the road, although occasional assaults on the camps have occurred and local residents have called for firmer action.

HIPPIE PEACE CONVOY, 1986

This demonstrated the problem of keeping convoys of wanderers under control and protecting farm and common land, while ensuring that Britain remains a land of freedom. Although the hippies posed no threat of violence, the Home Secretary called them 'brigands' and the Prime Minister said life would be made difficult for them. When police drove them off crown land at dawn, their vehicles and many of their possessions were confiscated. The law of trespass and the handling of communities needs urgent rethinking in the light of the convoy's story.

Q1 *The 1970s and the 1980s have seen a marked increase in confrontation between police and some sections of the public. Why? How do these clashes compare with those of the nineteenth century? What can be done to lower tension and reduce violence, and at the same time to maintain law and order? Is confrontation inevitable when huge numbers of people are involved?*

CHAPTER 9

The Twentieth Century – Part 2

1. THE COURTS

Having briefly explored policing and crime in the twentieth century, we now move on to the developments which have taken place in the courts.

COURT OF CRIMINAL APPEAL, 1907

The creation of this court made it possible for the first time to appeal against conviction and sentence. In other words, if an offender wanted to prove that the Quarter Sessions or Assizes were wrong in finding him guilty or had given him an unfair sentence, he could appeal to this court. Before this, conviction had been final unless the trial judge had felt that a point of law needed checking at the Court of Crown Cases Reserved (see p. 141). The Court of Criminal Appeal would look both at the evidence given at the person's trial and the way the trial judge had handled the trial. In short, it went far beyond a mere point of law, and dealt with evidence and trial conduct. Its members were the Lord Chief Justice and Queen's Bench judges. Appeal trials never have juries. In 1968 the Court's powers were transferred to the new Criminal Division of the Court of Appeal with its Lord Justice of Appeal hearing the cases. The Crown cannot appeal to it against an acquittal. Appeal from the Criminal Division can be made to the House of Lords' 'Law Lords'.

The grand jury system ended in 1933 and the old distinction between a felony and a misdemeanour went in 1967. The terms *indictable* (a serious case involving the need of an indictment charge to be presented to a grand jury and probably a jury trial) and *non-indictable* (a lesser offence which JPs can try summarily, that is without a jury or indictment) continued to be used. In some cases an accused has the right to ask for a serious non-indictable charge to be heard by a jury. Conversely, most indictable charges like theft and receiving, are heard without juries with the accused's consent. Today crimes are divided into four classes: 1st Class – treason, murder; 2nd Class – manslaughter, rape, mutiny, etc.; 3rd Class – burglary, robbery, theft, arson, assault; 4th Class – same as 3rd, but less serious instances. From 1967, majority verdicts of eleven to one or ten to two from a jury were acceptable, providing a judge agreed and the jury had failed to reach a verdict after at least two hours.

CROWN COURT ACT, 1971

By the 1960s it was clear that Assizes were held too infrequently and in towns which were sometimes inconvenient to reach. Quarter Sessions too was felt to be outdated. The increase in crime and the growth of free legal aid meant the courts were severely strained. The 1971 act abolished both courts and introduced the Crown Court system.

Crown Courts are arranged in three tiers in each of their six circuits. There are 90 centres within the six circuits. They were chosen as far as practicable to be within travelling distance of people's homes.

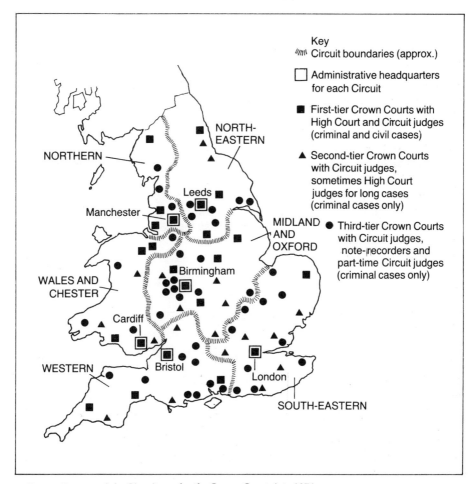

Crown Courts and the Circuits under the Crown Court Act, 1971

The third-tier courts try 3rd and 4th-Class crimes and are presided over by a Circuit Judge or a part-time Recorder, sitting with two to four JPs. A jury gives the verdict. The second-tier courts hear 3rd, 4th and 'simple' 2nd (those pleading 'guilty') Class crimes with the same personnel. A High Court judge may come to a second-tier court to hear a very lengthy 1st or 2nd-Class crime to save everyone else going miles to the first-tier court city. The first-tier courts hear all classes of crime. The High Court judges will come round regularly to hear the 1st and 2nd-Class ones while the 3rd and 4th-Class ones will be dealt with as for the second and third-tier courts.

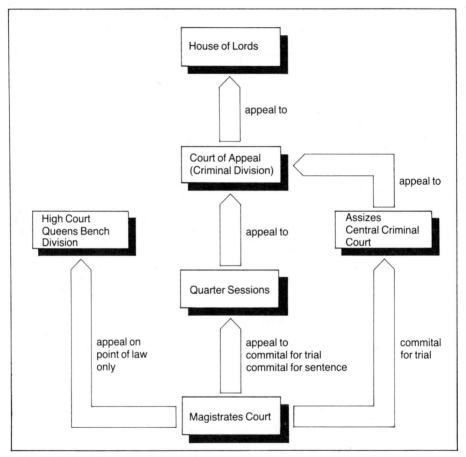

The criminal courts

Q1 *Make a collection of cuttings of Crown Court trials from newspapers. When you have a sufficient collection write an article about the work of each tier. Watch out for any appeals from those courts and try to follow what happens to them.*

The distinction between barristers and solicitors still continues, but solicitors can now be stipendiary magistrates (1948) and Circuit Judges (1971), which means they are now eligible to become full judges. They can also switch to being barristers if they take six to twelve months' training.

FREE LEGAL AID

Very often offenders do not have the money to pay for a solicitor or barrister. In 1903 the Poor Prisoners' Defence Act helped them if they were to be tried at Assize or Quarter Sessions. In 1930 this was extended to cover magistrates' court hearings. The present scheme was started by the Legal Aid Act, 1974. People apply to a local aid committee for a legal-aid certificate for which they have to declare what means they have. The problem is that with rising incomes many people fall just outside the limits allowed and so have to use up their own money fighting their case.

JURY SERVICE –
an explanatory leaflet

You are now about to become a juror. You are going to do a vitally important job. This leaflet explains what happens at a criminal trial and your part in it. [. . .]

WHY HAVE A JURY?
There is no fairer way of deciding facts than to take twelve people selected at random. Their job is to listen carefully to all that takes place during the trial and then to go to the juryroom and pool their experience, common sense and wisdom to reach a proper verdict. [. . .]

IN THE COURTROOM
THE JUDGE
The judge presides over the trial. He or she decides questions of law.
The jury decides questions of fact.

THE LAWYERS – WHAT DO THEY DO?
Prosecuting and defending counsel are barristers, who are instructed by solicitors. Prosecuting counsel is in court to present the case against the defendant as fairly as possible. He calls prosecution witnesses to give evidence and tests or 'cross-examines' defence witnesses.

Defence counsel is in court to test the prosecution and to present the case for the defence. He cross-examines prosecution witnesses to discover any weaknesses or contradictions in what they say. He must give them the opportunity to give their version of any matters which concern them and which will be raised by the defence later in the trial.

SWEARING-IN AND CHALLENGING
[. . .] If you know a defendant, a witness or anyone taking part in the trial or are in any way connected with the case, you must let a court official know before you have been sworn or have affirmed. If you become aware of a connection after the trial has begun, you should immediately send a note to the clerk of the court. [. . .]

SPEECHES AND SUMMING UP
After all the evidence has been heard prosecuting counsel sometimes makes a closing speech after which defending counsel addresses the jury.
The judge will then sum up. He will tell you what the law is. You must listen very carefully and follow his directions. He will then remind you of the evidence. It is often helpful to make notes during the summing up.

INSIDE THE JURY ROOM
At the end of the case an usher will swear to keep you all together until you reach your verdict. You will then be taken into the jury room and allowed no outside communication at all except by note to the clerk of the court. [. . .]

THE VERDICT
The verdict on each count must be unanimous: that is you must all agree.
There is such a thing as a majority verdict but this can be given only when the judge has called you back into court and said that he will accept such a verdict. The judge will not do this until some time has elapsed since you retired to consider your verdict. [. . .]

(From 'Jury service — an explanatory leaflet', 1984)

A leaflet explaining jury service

MAGISTRATES' COURTS

Magistrates try the vast majority of criminal cases. Apart from a few stipendiary (full-time lawyer) magistrates in very large cities, they are all volunteers who simply get their expenses paid. Women have been appointed magistrates since 1918. They sit in court at least once a fortnight and often hear 'matrimonial' cases on a separate day as well. If they are juvenile magistrates, that too increases their court work. Men and women from about the age of 30 years upwards are selected from the community by selecting committees whose members' names are not published so as to prevent any pressure being put upon them.

The selectors are often magistrates or ex-magistrates. They may approach likely candidates, or candidates may apply to the committee. Very thorough interviews are given to make sure that the candidates have not got any racial or class bias. Care is also taken to try to keep any political bias evenly balanced and to a minimum. Magistrates have to live within ten miles of their courts and be available at any time to deal with emergencies. The judicial system is completely dependent on them as professional judges could not cope without them.

Since the introduction of Crown Courts magistrates have had the added duty of taking it in turns to sit with the judges in those courts. In such trials the professional judge and the JPs confer together as to what sentence to give. Since 1966 newly appointed JPs have had to visit all the types of prison and centre which they can sentence people to. This is something which even professional judges do not have to do when appointed, although they might have been income-tax lawyers for years before becoming judges of criminals. Magistrates are given a course of legal booklets to read through, although they rely on their clerks to tell them precisely what the law is when need be.

As there are so many magistrates, it is essential that they try to standardise their sentencing for different offences. To do so they meet together periodically and do 'sentencing exercises'. JPs from different benches are put together into small groups and given the same difficult cases to fix sentences for. After each group has made its mind up, the groups report back to each other and compare their decisions.

Actual bodily harm

Chris and Ron, both aged seventeen, have pleaded guilty to this charge. The facts are:

With four of their friends they gate-crashed a dance which was being run in the Church Hall by the local youth club. The boys all had shaven heads and wore heavily steel-capped boots.

The dance was attended by young people aged fifteen to nineteen and was well run.

Two committee members saw what was happening and decided to ignore the intruders in the hope that if no one took any notice they would get bored and go away.

However, they grouped themselves around the disc jockey, a youth of eighteen, and started jeering at him. He told them to go away and let him get on with his job. One of the intruders grabbed the disc jockey by the lapels of his coat and butted him in the face. The disc jockey brought up his knee to free himself and then Chris hit him on the head with a coke bottle which did not break. He fell to the ground and while he was down Ron kicked him twice in the ribs.

A general fight ensued which was only ended by the arrival of the police. The disc jockey had a large bruise on his scalp and two broken ribs.

Social enquiry reports
Chris and Ron have been friends all their lives, living in the same area.

CHRIS – eldest of a family of six, his father is a labourer, his mother an office cleaner. He has little respect for his father and when in trouble his mother always covers up for him. He attended a comprehensive, was in the lowest stream, had a poor record and left at sixteen. He had a fair number of jobs, work record only fair due to poor time-keeping. Family is known to all local and council social agencies.

RON – youngest but one of a family of nine. His father is a labourer, often unemployed. Mother does not work. For many years there have been acute matrimonial troubles, due to father spending much time at the local pub and betting office. Often returns home under the influence of drink – habitually assaults his wife. At school Ron was described as average ability but in 'C' stream because of failure to use his intelligence – work record poor.

Left school at sixteen, worked as a builder's labourer. Work record only fair due to absenteeism, can work well when inclined.

At school, in the area where he lives and at work has been described as something of a bully.

Ron has always had a close relationship with his mother and in recent years there have been frequent rows with his father because his father treats his mother badly. The police have been called to the house on three occasions to stop them fighting.

Previous convictions
Chris – at fourteen, two years probation for theft of goods valued at £60.

Ron – at sixteen, fined £7 for malicious damage in the vestibule of a cinema where he and his friends were misbehaving.

Possibilities
Discharge; absolute or conditional. Fine – £1,000. Probation – one to three years. Youth custody – four to twelve months. Prison – six months. Detention centre – three to sixteen weeks.

2. TWENTIETH-CENTURY SENTENCING CHANGES

CAPITAL PUNISHMENT

The Homicide Act of 1957 divided murders into two categories: (a) *capital*; (b) *non-capital*. Capital covered killing during theft, while trying to avoid arrest, killing a policeman or prison officer and any second murder. All other killings were classed as non-capital. This arrangement proved very unsatisfactory. The act also brought in the idea of *diminished responsibility*, which meant that a person could not be convicted of murder if he or she were suffering from some abnormality of mind *at the time of the murder*. The person did not need to be permanently insane to enter such a plea.

The Murder (Abolition of Death Penalty) Act in 1965 made life imprisonment the alternative to hanging except for treason and violent piracy. This act was originally in force for a trial period, but in 1969 it was made permanent. During this period the murder figures were: 1966 – 122;

> **Q1** *What sentence would you impose in the sentencing exercise above? Check with your local JP to see if he or she agrees.*

1967 – 154; 1968 – 148; 1969 – 119; 1970 – 135. In the 1970s the prison population increased by 150 murderers a year who were serving life sentences. No prisoner serving life imprisonment is released without the Home Secretary's express order. Those who murder police or prison officers, commit terrorist murders or sexual or sadistic child murders, or kill with firearms serve at least twenty years. No one is supposed to be released who is a danger to the community.

The Argument for and against Hanging

For
1. A dead murderer cannot kill again.
2. It will deter other people.
3. A murderer in jail may escape.
4. It will save the money spent on a prisoner during life imprisonment.
5. A hanged murderer gets what he deserves.
6. Most people want to see murderers hanged.
7. Hanging protects police and prison staff.
8. Hanging satisfies the victim's relatives.

Against
1. The wrong person might be hanged.
2. It is not a deterrent as statistics show.
3. No one should take life, even the State.
4. It is asking too much of anyone to hang someone else.
5. It is against the teachings of different religions.
6. Even the worst person might be reformed.
7. Hanging makes martyrs of terrorists.
8. The murderer may be mentally ill or may have committed a 'domestic' murder and will never kill again.

CORPORAL PUNISHMENT

The 1914 Criminal Justice Act ruled that (a) no one was to be whipped more than once for one offence; (b) whippings were only allowed if a law about a particular offence actually said it was allowed for that offence. The 1948 Criminal Justice Act ended whippings as sentences of the court. Floggings were to continue for anyone causing a mutiny in prison or assaulting prison staff. The 1967 Criminal Justice Act ended even these floggings.

Q1 *Prepare a speech either for or against capital punishment.*

FINES

The 1914 Criminal Justice Act allowed 'time to pay'. The court could set a time limit for the fine's payment and prevent many people having to go to prison for failing to pay immediately. The Criminal Justice Act of 1982 did away with maximum fines for specific crimes and established five levels of fines which could be adjusted for inflation. Three years later, the fines were doubled.

Fine Levels	1982	1985
Level 1	£25	£50
Level 2	£50	£100
Level 3	£200	£400
Level 4	£500	£1000
Level 5	£1000	£2000

In 1983–4, £128 million was paid in fines, mostly for motoring offences.

In the 1980s 2 million fines are imposed each year, and 1,000 fine defaulters are in prison on an average day, amounting to 3 per cent of inmates. The Government is considering using community service orders (see p. 189) instead of prison for defaulters and keeping prison for those who *will not*, rather than *cannot* pay.

PREVENTIVE DETENTION

The 1908 Prevention of Crime Act gave courts power to give 'preventive detention', that is, sentences of up to ten years on top of sentences of three years or more to hardened criminals. This was to keep them out of society rather than deter them. These sentences were served at Camp Hill Prison, Isle of Wight, under a pleasant regime. The 1948 Criminal Justice Act ended penal servitude and hard labour. It replaced preventive detention with 'corrective training and preventive detention' for *recidivists* (people who commit crimes over and over), allowing two to four years for 17 to 29-year-olds and a maximum of fourteen years for those over 30. The 1967 Criminal Justice Act ended corrective training and substituted 'extended sentences' of up to ten years for frequent recidivists.

Q1 *What factors does a court take into consideration when an offender asks for time to pay?*

Q2 *Why is the adjustable level system better in an inflationary world than the old system of a maximum fine?*

Q3 *Why are fines the most cost-effective punishment? Are fines also reform-effective?*

Q4 *Can 'preventive detention' be justified?*

SUSPENDED SENTENCES

Since 1967 suspended sentences can be given. This means that the criminal does not go to prison unless he or she commits another offence during the suspension period. He or she has to serve the sentence plus receiving a punishment for the new offence if that happens.

CRIMINAL JUSTICE ACT, 1982 (EFFECTIVE 1983)

This act has two objectives: (1) to bring custodial care up to date and make it clear that custodial sentences should only be given in the last resort; (2) to improve the non-custodial orders the courts can make. Custodial sentences may be used if (a) the offender is unable or unwilling to respond to a non-custodial alternative; (b) if it is essential to protect the public from the offender; (c) the offence is so serious that the other options cannot be used. A social inquiry report is needed before a custodial sentence is given and the offender is entitled to legal help.

The act encourages courts to make offenders pay compensation to victims. Such payments are to come before any fine if the offender's means are limited. It also ends prison and borstal sentences for young offenders and substitutes detention and youth custody sentences (see pp. 189–90).

3. JUVENILES AND YOUNG PERSONS

The twentieth century has seen a major development in the handling of juveniles (ten to thirteen-year-olds) and young persons (fourteen to sixteen-year-olds). In 1908 the Children's Act banned prison sentences for those under fourteen years old and only allowed them for fourteen to sixteen-year-olds in rare cases. It started juvenile courts for people under seventeen. These courts are really special sittings of magistrates' courts.

But the Children's Act of 1908 (known as the 'Children's Charter') failed to lay down how many JPs should sit in a juvenile court. This meant that the number could vary widely from five to ten. The Committee on the Treatment of Young Offenders, which reported in 1927, said there must be a rule made on the number. It also argued that it was necessary to restrict other people being in the courtroom. It noted that sometimes 20 to 50 people, ranging from police to students, were there. The Committee felt that juvenile hearings should be as private as possible, and that the sittings should be in different buildings from those in which adult courts met. Nevertheless, a juvenile court, as the drawing opposite shows, is often a crowded place indeed.

> **Q1** *What are the advantages of suspended sentences?*

The Children and Young Persons Act, 1933, said nothing about separate premises or restricting 'other persons' from attending. It laid down that there should be two to three JPs hearing a case, one of whom had to be a woman. Juvenile JPs were to be annually elected from the JPs most suited for dealing with children. Simply having a 'love of children' was not sufficient. A juvenile magistrate had to fully appreciate a child's way of life and environment. Under the Justice of the Peace Act, 1949, they had to be under 50 years old (preferably 30 to 40 years old) when appointed and had to retire at 65 years old. The 1933 act required Local Education Authorities (LEAs) to produce reports on offenders as the 1927 Committee had complained of the courts' lack of information. The 1933 act also substituted the phrases, 'true or untrue' instead of a plea of 'guilty or not guilty', a 'finding of guilt' for 'conviction', and 'an order made upon such a finding' for 'the sentence'. These changes were to try and avoid a child thinking he or she had become a fully fledged criminal. In 1963, the Children and Young Persons Act was amended to include an order for parents or guardians to attend the court if required.

A Juvenile Court

Juvenile Courts' Special Features

1. The maximum number of magistrates is three, of whom one must be a woman.
2. They must be held on a different day from the normal court and usually in a different room.
3. The procedure must be as informal as possible.
4. Reporters are not permitted to reveal offenders' names, addresses or schools unless specifically allowed to do so.
5. There are no seats for the public.

CARE PROCEEDINGS AND CRIMINAL PROCEEDINGS

The 1969 Act laid down two procedures in juvenile courts: (a) *care proceedings* if it is thought the young person is beyond control; (b) *criminal proceedings* if the young person has committed a criminal offence.

Juvenile Courts

Procedures	Possible Court Decisions
Care Proceedings In need of care or beyond control. Babyhood upwards.	1. Payment of damages or compensation 2. Parents bound over to care for their child properly 3. Hospital or guardianship order 4. Care Order putting the child in the custody of the Local Authority 5. Supervision Order of up to three years under a Local Authority supervisor or probation officer
Criminal Proceedings Minimum age of criminal responsibility 1908–32 7 years 1933–62 8 years 1963–8 10 years 1969– 10 years, but between 10 and 14 years the prosecution has got to prove the child *knew* what was right or wrong Maximum age 1908–68 21 years 1969– 18 years	*Non-custodial* 1. Care Proceedings as above 2. Absolute Discharge 3. Conditional Discharge 4. Fine. Parents or guardians can be made to pay. 5. Compensation Order 6. Probation Order 7. Attendance Centre Order for 10+ year olds (14+ year olds, 1969). 12–36 hours in 2–3 hour Saturday sessions 8. Community Service Orders, 1972. 16+ year olds maximum of 120 hours *Custodial* 1. Approved School, before 1969 2. Borstal Training Order until 1982: 15–21 year olds (17–21 years, 1969), 6 months to 2 years 3. Detention Centre Orders: (a) 1969–82, 14+ year old boys, 3 months and a year's probation; (b) 1983 onwards, 17–21 year olds, 3 weeks to 4 months; tougher regime, 1985 4. Youth Custody Order, 1983 onwards, 15–20 year old boys and 17–20 year old girls, 4–12 months

APPROVED SCHOOLS AND COMMUNITY HOMES

In 1932 Reformatory and Industrial Schools became Approved Schools. They were divided into three age groups: junior, intermediate and senior. Their regime was fairly permissive and escape was easy. Three boys' schools specialised in nautical training, while others dealt with retarded pupils. Farming, building, engineering, etc., were taught too in 86 boys' and 35 girls' schools. The maximum sentence was three years or to school leaving age. Of those leaving approved schools between 1963 and 1967, 60 per cent were reconvicted. The Children and Young Persons Act, 1969, removed JPs' power to send children to them, replacing them by Care Orders. Community Homes replaced the schools for under seventeen year olds in 1973.

Lunchtime at an approved school

REMAND HOMES (REMAND CENTRES, 1948)

Children can be sent to these homes for reports to be made on them which enable the juvenile courts to decide what to do with them. Children under the care of the local authority may be sent to them for assessment even if they have not committed a crime.

BORSTALS

In 1902 an experiment in reformatory treatment was begun at Rochester Prison in the Kent village of Borstal to see if a treatment for young offenders could be developed. So successful was the experiment that the 1908 Prevention of Crime Act ordered similar places to be set up and courts given the power to sentence young people of fifteen to twenty-one years who persistently absconded from approved schools or committed serious offences to be sent to them for six months to two years. They would be released when their progress was satisfactory. In 1930 the first 'open' Borstal was started at Lowdham Grange near Nottingham.

Research at Dover Borstal in the 1970s showed that the longer inmates remained there the more likely they were to be reconvicted. Of those who left borstals in 1975, 85 per cent were reconvicted. The governor of Glen Parva Borstal, Leicestershire, summed it up when he said in 1978, 'You cannot take somebody and give him 42 weeks in borstal and put right eighteen or nineteen years of neglect, disturbance and deprivation'.

There was overcrowding in borstals, just as there was in prisons. Boys organised themselves and assigned key roles. A *daddy* was the tough who always got the use of the snooker table. His status was based on the number of *joes*, the weak ones, who slaved for him. *Cheesers* were those who sucked up to the staff. In 1969 the minimum age was raised to seventeen years and then borstals were abolished in 1982.

Huntercombe Borstal, Oxfordshire

Weekday Timetable

06.45 cells unlocked	14.00 work parade
07.30 breakfast	16.30 cease work; tea
08.15 work parade	17.15 lock up; staff tea
12.00 cease work; lunch	18.00 classes commence
12.30 lock-up so staff can	18.30 association commences
have lunch	20.45 association ceases
13.45 unlock	21.00 roll call; lock up

Numbers: 194 inmates
Meals: three cooked meals a day; breakfast, dinner, tea (supper – *one* of cake, cheese, meat rolls or buns)
Work: farming, painting, decorating, bricklaying, plastering, concrete moulding of garden sheds, cable covers, learning 'bedsit cookery', helping in OAP home or in psychiatric hospital
Out of cell time: 11 hours 15 minutes

PROBATION SERVICE – PROBATION ACT, 1907

In the 1840s Matthew Hill, Recorder of Birmingham, started an unofficial register of people willing to supervise offenders. By 1907 there were 144 'Police Court missionaries', when the official Probation Service began. From then on courts could put people 'on probation', although they were not compelled to appoint probation officers until 1925. The 1982 Criminal Justice Act gave the courts power to make offenders on probation do certain activities or not do others and attend *day centres* for up to 60 days. There their problems could be tackled, talks attended and help given. In recent years there has been a marked decline in the use of probation. Some say it is because probationers are found to re-offend at the same rate as those who are fined or imprisoned. Others say that courts used to give probation as a 'mercy' sentence to first offenders to keep them out of prison, but no longer do so. Community service is proving more cost-effective though no better at reforming.

ATTENDANCE CENTRES

The Criminal Justice Act of 1948 provided for local attendance centres for ten to twenty-one-year-olds who had broken probation orders or committed an offence for which an adult could have been sent to prison. Maximum attendance in two or three hour sessions is twelve hours for ten to fourteen-year-olds, 24 hours for fifteen to sixteen-year-olds and 36 hours for seventeen to twenty-one-year-olds, on Saturday afternoons. The centres are run by volunteers such as senior policemen, school-teachers, etc., and they meet in youth clubs or halls. There are junior and senior centres for boys and junior ones for girls; a few are mixed. The Criminal Justice Act of 1982 said they must be 'reasonably accessible'. This meant ten miles or 45 minutes' travelling time for under fourteen-year-olds and fifteen miles or $1\frac{1}{2}$ hours' travelling time for those over fourteen. Attenders have to pay any fares.

COMMUNITY SERVICE ORDERS

In 1972 courts were given the power to serve community service orders to make offenders do a spell of useful unpaid work. A sixteen-year-old (the minimum age) can be sentenced to a maximum of 120 hours. There are signs that the system has proved highly successful for old offenders, but also that it has little deterrent effect on others. It is certainly more cost-effective than probation. Some 15,720 orders were made in 1979 and 30,830 in 1982. Half of them would otherwise have been put in custody.

DETENTION CENTRES (1948 ONWARDS)

The aim of these centres is to give male offenders usually three to sixteen weeks of short, sharp treatment. In 1985, there were 1,500 offenders in junior and senior centres, although 2,202 places were available. Detention centres are not suitable for offenders with mental or physical disabilities. A tougher regime was introduced in March, 1985, when the Home Secretary said:

> 'The importance of the impact on offenders of the first few days of a detention centre sentence has been confirmed . . . [so] the initial two-week programme will be particularly brisk . . . Greater emphasis will be placed on parades and inspections. High standards of cleanliness, tidiness, discipline and personal effort will be required.'

It is not known whether this treatment will work. Some 75 per cent of those who left in 1975 became recidivists. In 1986 the Prison Inspectors and the Magistrates' Association condemned the treatment.

Q1 *Find out (a) what work offenders do in your area; (b) where and when they meet; (c) who supervises them.*

YOUTH CUSTODY ORDERS

The 1982 Criminal Justice Act abolished prison and borstal sentences for young offenders and substituted short Detention Centre sentences or longer Youth Custody ones where other non-custodial punishments were not suitable, for fifteen to twenty-year-old boys and seventeen to twenty-year-old girls. The sentences were for four to twelve months, followed by three to twelve months' supervision.

Youth Custody is designed for violent persons, hooligans, those who attack pub owners and bus drivers or who injure, riot, loot or steal vehicles; it is also for persons who may drink or take drugs, and who are unskilled and immature. It is designed to punish such people and instil self-respect, self-discipline and social behaviour. It does have the advantage of getting them away from their bad environment. It makes them keep themselves clean and healthy and keeps them working under discipline. They get personal attention from the staff. This is intended to enable them to cope with life more successfully when they leave. The disadvantages are that they make contact with other offenders and become resentful at being depersonalised. They may find it difficult to get a job when they leave. Most sentences given are for six months. They can earn remission of one-third of their sentences for good behaviour.

4.   PRISONS IN THE TWENTIETH CENTURY

OPEN PRISONS

In 1936 New Hall Camp was opened for 50 men as an 'annexe' to Wakefield Prison. The men lived in dormitory huts and worked on farms or made boots. The British idea of the 'open prison' had begun.

After World War II open prisons were started as a way of relieving pressure on overcrowded closed ones. It was cheap to buy up and run a disused armed forces' camp.

Unfortunately open prisons began as an emergency measure without an adequate set of prison rules to guide them. If this had been done it would be easier to fit them into life with the communities around them. Many are run like closed prisons, even though they have no perimeter walls. Some argue that this makes them a soft option for Category D prisoners (see p. 193). Others do not agree. They say a prisoner in an open prison faces a kind of mental barrier rather than a stone one.

Q1   *Why is 'open prison' a contradiction in terms? In what ways is it*
     (a) 'open'; (b) a 'prison'?

Q2   *Why does an open prison need fewer staff than a closed one?*

The buildings are often very basic wartime huts held together by paint and the inmates are last in the queue for the 'foam mattress issue'. Set in rural areas they are more difficult for relatives to reach than local prisons in towns.

Staff have found that it is as much a problem to keep prying outsiders out as it is to keep inmates in! This has sometimes made staff over-protective to the inmates and over-suspicious of the public view of open prisons.

Often prisoners work at local factories or firms. The money they earn goes to the Treasury and not, as one might expect, to their families. They visit local church services, help at fetes, field teams against local ones, entertain Old Age Pensioners (OAPs) etc. Unfortunately the Home Office attitude has been largely discouraging to these prisons.

For the Home Office, open prisons simply solve an overcrowding problem and are merely the 'ones without walls'. However, the May Report in 1979 (see p. 196) said it was extraordinary that greater use was not made of them. One open prison governor pinpointed the problem when he wrote that such hopeful developments as open prisons fell foul of the public, who are angry and depressed by violence and laziness, the hostile press, timid politicians and unimaginative civil servants. He added that some politicians demanding 'tougher measures' overlook the lack of resources, (in 1981 an electronic cell block cost £20,000 per inmate), while other politicians were disbelieved when they argued that shorter sentences could be as effective as long ones. In any event, the main use for open prisons in the future will probably be for short-sentence first offenders and those about to be released after long terms in closed prisons.

THE PRISON CRISIS AND HOW IT AROSE

Prison Population for England and Wales, 30 August 1985 (NACRO)

Males		Females	
Remand Centres	3,748	Open prisons	349
Local prisons	17,207	Closed prisons	1,019
Closed training prison	13,159	Closed Youth Custody	
Open prisons	3,404	Centres	120
Closed Youth Custody		Open Youth Custody	
Centres	5,458	Centres	89
Open Youth Custody		*Senior Detention Centres*	1,016
Centres	1,016	*Other Detention Centres*	1,560
Total Population	48,145	Total Capacity	39,804

Q1 *Would the 'mental barrier' be a serious problem to a prisoner in an open prison, or an aid to adjusting to a new life?*

Q2 *What arguments can you produce for the Home Office giving a higher priority to open prisons?*

The 1898 Prisons Act looked forward to a fresh start in the twentieth century. In August of 1985 the prison population reached 48,000, a crisis situation. What has gone wrong?

In 1908 prison for children was ended and borstal training begun. In 1921 convict hair-cropping and broad arrows on uniforms were stopped. Warders became known as prison officers and were given formal training. In 1948 penal servitude and the old classifications were ended. 'Humane containment' by *corrective training* was the new policy. Instead of controlling prisoners by the 'treatment' of separation, the controlling would be by 'humanising' them towards a normal life. TV, good food and sympathetic handling were to be part of the means. Psychologists' and psychiatrists' services would be available. Ordinary people were welcome as Prison Visitors and allowed to get to know prisoners allocated to them by the governor. All this brings us back to the root problem which the authorities faced in 1898. What should a prison be trying to do?

Firstly, it is the State's method of providing a punishment which will satisfy the demand for revenge of victims and society. Hopefully it will deter people from similar actions too. Secondly, it protects the public from dangerous people. Thirdly, it aims to reform the offender. The first two points require a strict and uniform regime, but the third does not. Reform can only be achieved if the inmates are treated as individuals and the staff get to know them. Any overcrowding, say three in a cell, makes this difficult to start with. A single person in a cell can develop his or her personality by arranging his or her belongings, keeping a caged bird, enjoying a degree of privacy, etc. Trades can be taught from cooking to metalwork. Dowty Engineering of Cheltenham gave metalwork machines to Gloucester Prison and offered to take ex-prisoners who had trained on them. Not only do such courses give prisoners new skills, but they provide an opportunity for good human relations. Today, however, overcrowding and staff shortages mean that much of the equipment lies idle and the prisoners remain in their cells up to 23 hours a day.

It is difficult to see how the lack of privacy and the urine bowl in the corner are going to enable three men in a cell to start a fresh life when they are discharged. The days of the late-eighteenth-century prisoner with his day and night cells in Gloucestershire prisons or the nineteenth-century prisoner with his washbasin and toilet are, it seems, gone for ever. 'Slopping out' cannot be done by every prisoner simultaneously at reveille as the sewers will not take the strain. In 1971, discharging sewage from Liverpool Prison forced open nearby manhole covers on two occasions.

Q1 *Explain and comment on what Sir Alex Patterson, new Prison Commissioner in 1922, meant when he said, 'It must be clear from the outset to all concerned that it is the sentence of imprisonment and not the treatment accorded in prison, that constitutes the punishment. Men come to prison as a punishment, not for punishment.'*

Overcrowding increased with the abolition of the death penalty in 1965, which led to more prisoners serving life sentences: 122 in 1957, 1,436 in 1978; 1,533 (including 49 women) in 1980. Life sentences, too, are given for manslaughter, rape, arson, and armed robbery, as well as murder. Tension has increased since the 1960s. Anti-suicide nets are strung between galleries, and men's ties are designed to snap at 18 kg.

In 1966 Lord Mountbatten headed an inquiry following the escape of the spy George Blake who was serving 42 years. He recommended four categories of prisoner according to security risk. Category A (highly dangerous) to D (fit for an open prison life). He supported the prison officers' call for a special prison in which to *concentrate* 120 most dangerous prisoners. It would be on the Isle of Wight and called Vectis (Roman for Wight). Within a strong perimeter wall he hoped there could be a reasonable regime. *Security* became the key word and *rehabilitation* became a lower priority. Category A prisoners would be liable to regular strip searches and minute checks of their property. They would also have to be escorted wherever they went.

Overcrowding in today's prisons

But at the same time the Advisory Committee on the Penal System recommended the *dispersal* of dangerous prisoners around selected prisons. When this was endorsed by the Radzivowicz Report in 1968, it was put into practice. Seven prisons were given specially strengthened sections and each received 30 to 60 Category A prisoners. The people who wanted the *dispersal* policy overlooked the fact that these dangerous men would exploit the weaker inmates and that two different security regimes would need to be run in a single prison. In the 1970s electric gadgets, TV cameras, floodlighting and dog patrols became common features of these prisons. Despite these features, though, some of the new dispersal prisons were an improvement on existing prisons. At Long Lartin, near Evesham, a modern prison for 250 Category A prisoners, cells have intercoms so that inmates can ask to go to the toilet day and night, and there is no longer 'slopping out'!

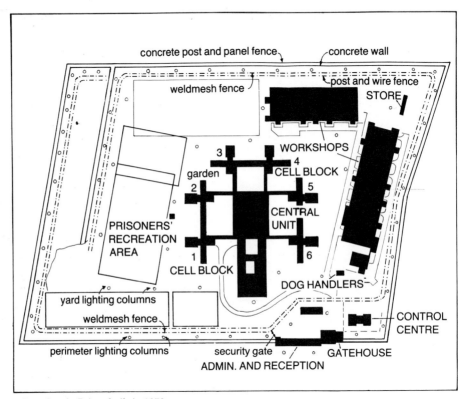

Long Lartin Prison built in 1972

RIOTS AT DISPERSAL PRISONS

Rioting began in the late 1960s at Parkhurst. A brief report blamed the disturbance on putting disturbed and difficult prisoners together. This highlighted one of the weaknesses of the dispersal policy. Albany Prison had tried to let dispersal prisoners mix with others, but had had to abandon this practice.

> **Q1** *List the defences for keeping dispersal prisoners inside. What type of prisoners are 'dispersal prisoners'?*

In 1972 large-scale escape plans were found at Albany and at Gartree Prisons. Rioting spread from those prisons to 39 others. In 1975 the Cabinet rejected Home Secretary Jenkins' secret plan to dramatically cut the prison population by 4,000 by granting early remission. The Cabinet thought judges would simply increase the length of sentences. Then, in 1976, serious rioting at another dispersal prison, Hull, occurred. It lasted for four days. Prison officers were injured and pinned down in parts of the prison and £$\frac{3}{4}$ million's worth of damage was done. The Home Office admitted that the prison held an abnormally high number of Category A prisoners (IRA, murderers, rapists) and the daily regime had had to be curtailed due to lack of staff available and a shortage of money to pay them for more overtime duty.

A four-day public inquiry by a reputable team was held in Conway Hall, London, to hear allegations that some staff had beaten up prisoners and destroyed their belongings the day after the riots ended. In 1979, eight officers were given suspended sentences by the crown court for assault. The report on this riot gave details about *Segregation Units* in dispersal prisons. They consisted of (a) Special Cells with no furniture or fittings for those being punished and (b) Reinforced Cells with strengthened walls, floors and bars for Category A prisoners. Although a governor could only put a prisoner in them for 24 hours, the Home Secretary or Board of Visitors could put them there month by month. These units meant that there were, in effect, prisons within prisons.

A *Control Unit* for persistently troublesome prisoners to serve doses of 180 days at a time was tried in Wakefield Prison for a year in 1974 and then abandoned in the face of strong criticism. How far should control go? Will an over-controlled person ever be able to readjust to the world? Yet, weak prisoners need control to support them, while disruptive ones need to be tamed.

The spectre of Russian political prisoners springs to mind at the mention of drugged prisoners. This issue is going to be a persistent one now that drugs can reduce the sex offender's urges and calm the psychopath. Sometimes prisoners ask for such drugs so that they can cope with themselves and live a normal life. It is pointed out that the use of drugs can reduce the need to use strait-jackets or other protective measures. It can even be argued that as the DHSS will not, and cannot, cope with those in need of hospital treatment, so use has to be made of drugs in overcrowded prisons.

Q1 *Should drugs be used to control prisoners? Would they violate human rights by modifying human behaviour?*

Q2 *Discuss when drugs should or should not be used in prison. What safeguards should there be?*

PRISON OFFICERS' PROTEST, 1978

In October 1978 prison governors warned the Home Secretary that, 'total breakdown is imminent in the prison system'. A pay claim revealed the deep-seated frustration of the prison officers who felt their problems had long been ignored. They had to spend their lives in the 'penal slums' which prisoners only stayed in for a while. Overtime averaged fourteen hours a week and often more. Nervous breakdowns and marriage problems were growing more common. They felt frustrated in any efforts to reform prisoners because of overcrowding and staff shortages.

When overtime, and hence pay, was cut back in a government economy drive the prison officers started industrial action. This meant prisoners were not taken to court for trials, exercise stopped and workshops closed down. They felt the Home Office's Prison Board, set up in 1963, was unsympathetic to their grievances. Its popular Inspector-General, Brig. Maunsell, resigned when he realised he had no powers. The setting up of four Regional HQs in the 1960s had led to some local developments and initiatives, but this had led to staff and prisoners wanting to serve in what they considered the 'best' regions. 'Humane containment', it was felt, had reduced prison officers to zoo keepers. The Home Secretary appointed Justice May to head an immediate inquiry. The urgency of the situation was underlined by the need to use a MUFTI (Minimum Use of Force Tactical Intervention) squad with helmets and shields to quell a riot at Wormwood Scrubs on 31 August 1979. Later the police were called in to investigate complaints of prison officers assaulting inmates.

THE MAY REPORT, OCTOBER, 1979

The importance of this report is that it brought together all the current suggestions about what should be done. It told the DHSS that it must cope with the mentally disturbed then in prisons, but doubted the DHSS's promise to have 1,000 beds ready by 1985. It said the Prison Department should have a higher standing in the Home Office. It did not please the prison staff by saying that it wanted to play down the 'ex-military' background they tended to come from. Some governors and staff like the disciplinary approach used by former members of the armed forces as it keeps prisons under control. Others say it leads to confrontation.

The report said 'positive or purposive [useful] custody' should replace 'humane containment' as the main policy. It wanted to stress *reform*. It was against the concentration of Category A prisoners. It said prisons should be open to inspection by HM Factory and Public Health Inspectors. The Public Health Inspectors had been turned away from trying to inspect unhealthy conditions in April, 1979. It pointed to the need for an enormous new building programme. Fourteen new prisons for 6,622 prisoners are to be built by 1991. Prison designing still shows surprising faults. The lake planned for Felton Borstal had to be cancelled as inmates were liable to drown in it; the suspended ceiling at

Featherstone Prison had to be taken down to prevent inmates hiding things; Frankland Prison intended for Category A prisoners was found to have playing fields suitable for a helicopter snatch escape!

As noted previously, in August 1985 there were 48,145 inmates in prisons in Britain (16 per cent of whom were awaiting trial) compared to 42,200 in 1984, in buildings designed to hold 39,804. In 1984 the Home Office had forecast 43,000 for 1985 and 49,000 for 1992. The prison population had reached its forecast size seven years earlier than expected. That meant that the prison population was rising by 216 a week in 1985 when the Home Secretary announced that the wartime Lindholme RAF Base near Doncaster would be hurriedly got ready to house 600 (later 1,000) Category C prisoners, for which 200 prison officers would be recruited at once. The announcement coincided with the Prime Minister's drive against drug dealers and soccer hooligans, which could well increase the prison population.

If the situation is to be got under control, it will need a new prison like Lindholme to be opened every month. At Leeds, Oxford and Leicester, the number of prisoners exceeds the capacity of the prisons by 100 per cent. The Prison Officers' Association claims that 5,000 new staff are needed. Fortunately the cool, wet summer of 1985 prevented the frustrations of being locked three to a hot cell for 23 hours a day from bursting into riots, although many minor incidents did occur. The Home Secretary has the power, under the 1982 Criminal Justice Act, to release non-violent prisoners in the last six months of their sentences (should a prison be destroyed by riot or fire), but he has refused to use it and so release 10,000 prisoners early. This is in spite of research showing that regardless of length of sentence 80 per cent become recidivists.

The long-simmering dispute between the Prison Officers' Association and the Home Office broke out again in 1986. This time, the guards threatened to take selective action, a tactic used successfully by the teachers in 1985–6; the spokesman for the prison guards noted that while this action would have maximum impact, it would not make the prisoners' lives so intolerable that riots would break out.

THE HIGH COSTS OF PRISON

The extent to which the public pays through taxes for the prison system may be seen by glancing at the 1983–4 statistics. A prisoner in a Category B training prison cost the taxpayer £12,428 a year only a few years ago. Inflation means an annual increase.

Average Weekly Cost per Person, 1983–4

Local prisons/remand centres	£216	Dispersal prisons	£478
Category B training prison	£239	Category C training prison	£178
Open adult prison	£144	Closed youth establishment	£254
Open youth establishment	£283	Female establishments	£330

A DAY IN A LOCAL PRISON
(from WEA's *Crime and Penal System* 1976)

A day in prison–It is not possible to cover all aspects of people's lives in prison because of the variety of prison establishments, but a day in a local prison–where offenders are sent straight from court and where many spend their whole sentence might go like this:

07.00	Cells are unlocked: many carry their chamber pots to 'slop them out' in a communal lavatory. Breakfast is collected and eaten in cells. Cells are relocked immediately breakfast has been collected.
08.45	Exercise–half an hour's walk with other prisoners in a circle in a yard: also a chance to use the lavatory.
09.15	Work for perhaps 2¼ hours (longer in 'training prisons').
11.45	Lunch–possibly at a table ('in association') but more likely off a tray in the cell. Cells relocked immediately after lunch has been collected.
14.15	Exercise–round the yard again.
14.45	Work for perhaps 2¼ hours.
17.00	Tea and something warm to eat.
18.00	Some return to cells, some have recreation, some go to classes two or three evenings a week.
20.00	Cells locked for the night. Tea and a bun.
22.00	Lights out, except for those with special permission to study.

Prisoners work a five day week. At weekends they may be in their cells for 23 hours a day with no classes, recreation, library or canteen. T.V. is commonly available only 2 or 3 evenings a week, and only up to about 8.30 p.m.

Cells and dormitories–73% of adult prison places are in cells. In the older prisons, cells normally measure 12 ft × 9 ft × 8 ft [3.66 m × 2.74 m × 2.44 m] with two, often three beds. The door has a Judas-hole and there is a single barred window. In addition there are a wooden chair and small table, a waterjug and a chamberpot with a lid. The remaining 27% of places are in dormitories. In open prisons, which are nearly all converted service camps, men sleep in dormitories of about 20. A very few modern prisons have remote control of cell locks, which allows the chamber pot to be dispensed with.

Hygienic provisions–Except in a few of the newest prisons, there are no lavatories in cells in England. In older prisons 6 lavatories per 100 men is not unusual. A bath may be taken once a week. Clean clothes are issued once a week and underwear may be changed twice. Bedlinen is changed once a week.

Clothing–Male prisoners must wear uniforms. Women prisoners wear their ordinary clothes.

Contact with the outside world–Visits and letters from a prisoner's family and friends and letters written to them from prison are strictly rationed and with very few exceptions, letters (incoming and outgoing) are also censored.

Punishment–Apart from major offences taken to the criminal courts, the more serious breaches of prison rules, such as attacking an officer or incitement to riot, are dealt with in private by Boards of Visitors. These are committees of informed 'laymen', including magistrates, approved by the Home Office to each prison. They have a dual function since they also hear complaints from prisoners against the prison staff. Minor offences are dealt with by the Governor. Punishments include loss of remission (all prisoners are normally allowed ⅓ remission of their sentences for good conduct), loss of earnings and confinement to a punishment cell (see below). Dietary restrictions, such as bread and water, were abolished on June 1974. The most serious punishment is loss of remission, in effect a lengthening of the sentence. Up to 28 days may be taken away by the Governor and up to 180 days by the Board of Visitors. In 1974, 17,845 prisoners, well over one-quarter of the total, were punished.

A punishment cell is the same size as an ordinary cell. During the day there is only one wooden chair and a Bible. At night an iron framed bed with mattress, sheets, pillow and blanket are brought in with the chamber pot.

EXTRACTS FROM CHIEF INSPECTOR OF PRISONS' 1981 REPORT

Some extracts from this recent report of 1981 read like pages from John Howard's *State of the Prisons* of 1777. For example, the facility for bathing at Leeds local prison is described as 'the least adequate'. For 1,200 or so prisoners, Leeds has sixteen baths and three showers in a dirty and primitive basement area. If that were not bad enough, the water supply is so variable that only four baths can be used at any one time and the showers cannot be used at all because they interrupt the flow of water to the baths! Leeds has accommodation for 624 prisoners, half the room it needs to house its inmates. Its 334 workshop places are available for three hours a day; three-quarters of the prisoners never work in them on any one day. The Inspector concluded that 'overcrowding overshadows everything else' so that the prison had to 'function like a production line'.

5. WOMEN IN PRISON IN THE TWENTIETH CENTURY

The forcible feeding of suffragettes imprisoned for acts of violence in their campaign to get the vote for women in the years before World War I was gruesome. Lady Constance Lytton, who disguised herself as a working woman 'Jane Warton', described what happened to her in Liverpool Prison in 1911 when she was twenty-one and had not eaten for four days:

'The Senior Medical Officer said, "That is too long, I shall have to feed you, I must feed you at once," but he went out and nothing happened until about 6 o'clock in the evening, when he returned with . . . five wardresses and the feeding apparatus. He urged me to take food voluntarily. I told him that was absolutely out of the question . . . He did not examine my heart nor feel my pulse . . . I offered no resistance . . . but lay down voluntarily on the plank bed. Two of the wardresses took hold of my arms, one held my head and one my feet. One wardress helped to pour the food. The doctor leant on my knees as he stooped over my chest to get at my mouth. I shut my mouth and clenched my teeth . . . The doctor offered me the choice of a wooden or steel gag; he explained . . . that the steel gag would hurt and the wooden one not, and he urged me not to force him to use the steel gag. But I did not speak nor open my mouth, so that after playing about for a moment or two with the wooden one he finally had recourse to the steel. He seemed annoyed at my resistance and he broke into a temper as he plied my teeth with the steel implement. He found that on either side at the back I had false teeth mounted on a bridge which did not take out. The . . . wardress asked if I had any false teeth, if so, that they must be taken out; I made no answer . . . He dug his instrument down on the sham tooth, it pressed fearfully on the gum. He said if I resisted so much with my teeth, he would have to feed me through the nose. The pain of it was intense and at last I must have given way for he got the gag between my teeth, when he proceeded to turn it much more than necessary until my jaws were fastened wide apart, far more than they could naturally go. Then he put down my throat a tube which seemed to me much too wide and was something like four feet in length. The irritation of the tube was excessive. I choked the moment it touched my throat until it had got down. Then the food was poured in quickly; it made me sick a few seconds after it was down and the action of the sickness made my body and legs double up, but the wardresses instantly pressed back my head and the doctor leant on my knees. The horror of it was more than I can describe. I was sick over the doctor and wardresses, and it seemed a long time before they took the tube out . . . When the doctor had gone . . . I lay quite helpless. The wardresses were kind and knelt round to comfort me, but there was nothing to be done . . .'

Women's Social and Political Union's medal given to suffragettes for going on hunger strikes

Lady Constance lost 0.9 kg a day and her heart was damaged. She was one of those awarded the suffragette medal. One woman was force-fed 232 times.

The government tried to avoid this force-feeding by the Temporary Discharge for Ill-Health Act, 1913. It was known as the 'Cat and Mouse Act' as it involved releasing suffragettes when they became ill from refusing to eat and then re-arresting them after they had recovered at home.

Operation of the Cat and Mouse Act

At the time of the passing of the Act there were thirteen persons in prison:

	Date when sentenced	Offence	Sentence	Release	Remarks
	1913				
1	Jan. 9	Attack on letterbox	8 months	Aug. 20	Sentence served.
2	Feb. 7	Breaking windows	5 months	June 9	Sentence served.
3	Feb. 21	Breaking windows	6 months	July 18	Sentence served.
4	Feb. 21	Breaking windows	4 months	April 30	Discharged when sentence half served; no reason given.
5	Mar. 5	Firing a pillar box	9 months	April 28	Rearrested Aug. 1913, Jan., June 1914.
6	Mar. 8	Setting fire to railway carriage	9 months	April 28	Forcibly fed 114 times.
7	Mar. 20	Breaking windows	5 months	July 29	Served sentence.
8	Mar. 27	Breaking windows	1 month	End of April	Served sentence.
9	April 4	Attempted arson, Roehampton	4 months	July 18	Served sentence.
10	April 12	Found at Mitcham in possession of inflammatory materials	6 weeks	End of April	Not rearrested.
11			6 weeks	April 28	Rearrested, Jan. 1914.
12	April 22	Damaging pictures at Manchester Art Gallery	5 months	May 21	Not rearrested.
13			9 months	End of June	Not rearrested.

Date	Outrage	Damage (£)	Reported in	Date	Arrests	Sentence	Remarks
1914							
Feb. 22	Pavilion destroyed, Surbiton	1,000	Surrey Comet	Feb. 25			
Feb. 24	Redlynch House destroyed, Somerset	40,000	Western Gazette	Feb. 27			
Feb. 25	Windows smashed, Edinburgh	Small	Scotsman	Feb. 26			
Feb. 26	Whitekirk destroyed, East Lothian	10,000	The Times	Feb. 27			
Mar. 1	Church doors defaced, Birmingham	Slight	Birmingham Daily Post	Mar. 2			
Mar. 1	Bomb explosion, St. John's, Westminster	Slight	The Times	Mar. 2			
Mar. 1	Pavilion fired, Birmingham	Slight	Birmingham Daily Post	Mar. 2			
Mar. 1	'Golden Lion' fired, Birmingham	Slight	Birmingham Daily Post	Mar. 2			
Mar. 2	Screen damaged, St. John's, Edinburgh	Value of screen, 450	The Times	Mar. 3			
Mar. 3	Golf-links damaged, Bath	Not stated	Bath and Wilts Chronicle	Mar. 3			Released April 6, after forcible feeding.
Mar. 5	Cornricks destroyed, Bath	450	Bath Herald	Mar. 6			Rearrested May 20; released May 25, after forcible feeding.
Mar. 10	Rokeby Venus mutilated	Value of picture, 45,000	The Times	Mar. 11	Miss Richardson (a 'mouse')	6 months Mar. 12	Rearrested June 6; released July 28. Afterwards underwent operation.

POLLING BOOTH.

COMPANIONS IN DISGRACE.

Convicts and Women kindly note,   When once the harmful man of crime,
Are not allowed to have the vote;   In Wormwood Scrubbs has done his time,
The difference between the two   He at the poll can have his say,
I will now indicate to you.   The harmless woman *never* may.

C. H.

Printed and Published by the Artists' Suffrage League,   *A pro-suffragette cartoon*
259, King's Road, Chelsea.

In 1970 a new Holloway Prison for women was planned, more as a hospital than a prison. Pleasantly coloured square cells allow the prisoners to decide where to put their beds. They have light switches which the inmates can operate. Flush toilets and washbasins are included. Groups of cells, twelve, sixteen or twenty, can be arranged as required by shutting off sections. Groups of sixteen cells are to be run as 'families' with one inmate running the 'house'. Each member is to take this in turn and so learn to cater for the rest.

Old lags, however, prefer the old Holloway Prison where they can meet friends at the Centre where the wings met. The new prison has no centre point or wings, but is arranged in self-contained units. Staff sometimes

Q1   *Explain in your own words what the cartoon is saying.*

feel cut off from colleagues in them too. Built along the lines of a housing estate rather than an institution, it seems to produce the same undesired isolation that many housing estates do. In the event it does not seem to have succeeded. Serious concern was expressed in 1985 when some inmates under particular restraint mutilated themselves in their despair. Mothers may keep their babies there until they are one year old. At Askham Grange Open Prison they are allowed to keep their child until it is three years old. Today, there is one female prisoner for every 42 males in prison.

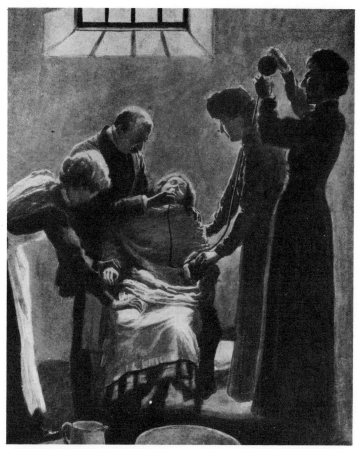

The forcible feeding of a suffragette

Q1 *Can forcible feeding ever be justified? What are the alternatives? Find out what happened when IRA prisoners died rather than eat.*

Q2 *If you had been designing a new Holloway would you have kept the nineteenth-century idea of wings meeting at a centre point or gone in for self-contained units? Can you suggest any alternative?*

Q3 *Why should far fewer women be in prison than men?*

CHAPTER 10

Trends and Conclusions

Crime and punishment have their roots in the customs of any society. Blood-feuds and the law of retaliation were centred round the family and the community. But just as parents teach children how to behave, be fair and curb their impulses for the family's general good, so the ruler would put restrictions on his subjects for the nation's general good. The community would catch, try and punish the offender. Laws would be made so that all knew what was a crime and what was not. This led rulers to set up a system of government which made them all-powerful. In this system there were three aspects of crime control:

1. Law making (legislating);
2. Law administering (executive work);
3. Judging lawbreakers (judicial work).

Anyone who controlled all three of these branches of government was an absolute ruler or dictator. He could make anything into a crime, send his men after the culprits and make sure his judges found them guilty.

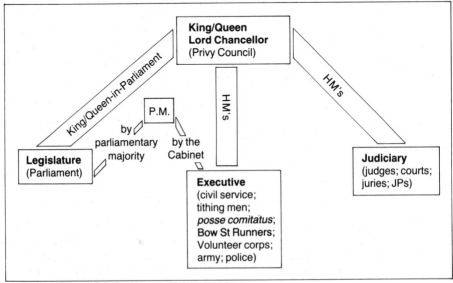

The Three Branches of Power

Although medieval and Tudor rulers held this absolute power, aided by their Lord Chancellors, the rise of Parliament was a challenge to the Stuarts. By the eighteenth century the judges could no longer be dismissed at the mercy of the ruler. Both Houses of Parliament had to petition the king to remove a judge. A new and powerful figure appeared, too, in the prime minister. Gradually the prime minister pushed the ruler into the background, but in theory the prime minister could not be a dictator as he only controlled two of the three branches of power. Let us see though, how this worked out in practice. The way it worked out explains our freedom today.

To oppose a Tudor king and his Lord Chancellor could be fatal. Heads fell without fair trials. To oppose an eighteenth-century prime minister, however, was possible. In the 1794 treason trials of those allegedly threatening the country's government, the juries were carefully chosen (see pp. 88–9). Nevertheless, Matthew Whiting and his fellow jurymen did not accept the government's case and voted for acquittal. In 1985 the trials took place of those miners accused of rioting at Orgreave in 1984. Margaret Thatcher's government had always stressed that it was strongly for 'law and order', yet it was the *prosecution* who withdrew the riot charges to end the trial before the jury retired. Looking back, we can discern a trend in the outcomes. The ruler won easily in Tudor times. He (and his prime minister) lost in 1794 in spite of every manoeuvre possible. In 1985 the prime minister did not attempt to interfere in the courts at all. The trend is thus towards democracy, and away from authoritarian rule or dictatorship.

Although 'evil acts' are *always* accepted as *crimes*, other crimes depend on the age people live in. In Tudor times rulers ordered one to worship in a certain way; in the eighteenth and nineteenth centuries society's leaders in Parliament and on the bench protected their property with Game Laws and executions for sheep stealing. In the twentieth century, society's leaders and the MPs and JPs (both now men and women from all 'classes') made the welfare of all the top priority. Laws had to protect everybody. Crimes against one person were crimes against all persons.

Catching the criminal over the centuries depended on whether there were good roads, and easy transport and communication. Without such facilities, committing crimes and criminal catching could only be achieved on a local level. The community was involved with its tithing men and the hue and cry. Gradually the King's Peace was extended over the country and the sheriff's *posse comitatus* was added to the local systems. *Amercement* and *murdrum* made communities take action.

This arrangement was followed by the practice of taking one's turn as a parish constable and the use of watchmen – 'Right Charleys' as some of them were. Thief-takers operated against little resistance from the law in the eighteenth century until Bow Street Runners were started. These new policemen were backed up by volunteer corps and the army when needed. The nineteenth century saw the appearance of civilian police forces over the country. This reduced the need to call on the troops. Today, the police use the latest technology in the fight against crime. 'Special' constables, commercial security forces (for example, Securicor) and community self-help arose on the side of law and order.

When it comes to trials, the citizen has played a key role. The magistrates, their courts and juries are as vital as ever. The rulers' judges coming round on circuit have for centuries held the court system together. But since 1701 they have not been under the political power of the ruler. Blood-feuds have given way in turn to compurgation, trials by ordeal, sanctuary, grand and petty juries, and an appeal system. Juveniles are now treated differently from adults. Free legal aid is available, at least for some. The trend here has been for fairer trials. Torture and the denial of a lawyer for the accused have long since vanished from the British scene.

The public exhibition of punishment has gone. Public executions, pillories, stocks, ducking stools and public whippings are no more. Public humiliation as a means of deterring criminals has been abandoned. Criminals are now kept out of sight while doing probation or serving time in prison. Fines continue as always, but community service orders have now appeared with new ways for criminals to pay their debts to victims. Punishments are now more designed to suit the criminal than they once were. The use of prison for simply holding a person awaiting trial, or subsequently awaiting execution, has given way to imprisonment as a punishment in itself. The neglect of prisoners in communal prisons in the seventeenth and eighteenth centuries gave way to purpose-built, rule-run, staff-trained establishments in the nineteenth century, as experiment after experiment was made in designing prisons and laying down their daily regimes. Hulks and transportation came and went. So too did pointless tasks such as shot drill. Now we have open prisons and dispersal prisons; but overcrowding increases to a worrying degree. The reforming of inmates has had a varied history. Its future, like its past, seems uncertain.

Children, once treated like adults, are now dealt with by an elaborate system based on a juvenile court with a wide variety of committal orders.

Domestic crime has always existed and will continue to do so. Crime related to poverty rises and ebbs with economic decline and growth. Greed continues to affect the crime rate, whose growth is checked partially by law and partially by current moral standards. Different types of crime and criminals arise. The highwaymen are replaced by suburban thieves. Computers as well as homes are broken into.

Crime is not so much *against* society as *within* society. It is a form of social behaviour which some members turn to for a variety of reasons. Criminals have their behaviour standards for the most part too.

Questions persist. Does TV cause crime? Are the streets today less safe than they were in the nineteenth century?

Each generation tolerates people in different ways but has got to live with them. The important thing is to make sure (a) there are laws stating what is criminal and what is not, (b) there is a civilian, non-political policing organisation, (c) there is a fair trial system, and (d) there is a set of alternative punishments which satisfy the victim and the community, warn off future criminals and do what can be done to reform the convicted.

By and large the British system has come out well on most, though perhaps not all, accounts. Civilisation has taken away the public display of brutality involved in the punishment of crime and done what it can to relate the punishment to the individual as an human being. But that has not removed crime from the community and it is unlikely that any country will ever succeed in doing that.

Theme Guide

To follow a theme, study the chapter (e.g.[1]) and section (e.g.2) in chronological order throughout the book.

LAW MAKING [1] 2; [2] 4; [3] 4; [4] 1; [7] 14, 15, 16; [9] 1, 2, 4.

CRIME, RIOTS, KEEPING ORDER, ETC. [3] 1; [4] 2, 7; [5] 1,3; [6] 2, 3, 6, 7.

CAUSES OF CRIME [1] 1; [6] 7; [7] 3, 4, 6, 7, 16.

CRIME PREVENTION, POLICING [2] 2; [3] 3, 4; [4] 4, 6; [5] 2; [6] 1,2,5; [7] 8,9,10, 11; [8] 1.

COURTS [3] 5, 13; [4] 4,5; [7] 15; [9] 1.

TRIALS [2] 3; [3] 2, 8, 10, 11; [4] 2, 5; [5] 3; [7] 12.

JURIES [3] 6, 12; [9] 1.

JPs [3] 2; [4] 4, 5; [5] 2; [7] 13; [9] 1,3.

PUNISHMENT: PRISONS [3] 7; [6] 9; [7] 16; [9] 4.

PUNISHMENT: ALL OTHER PUNISHMENTS [2] 1; [3] 14, 15, 16; [6] 8; [7] 14; [9] 2, 3.

Q1 *Is crime inevitable in all societies?*

Q2 *'Prison solves nothing as recidivism shows.' Discuss. What would you do to solve the present prison population crisis?*

Index